Your System's Sweetspots: CEO's Advice on Basic Cyber Security

CEO's Advice on Computer Science

Warren H. Lau

Published by INPress International, 2023.

YOUR SYSTEM'S SWEETSPOTS: CEO'S ADVICE ON BASIC CYBER SECURITY

First edition. March 27, 2023.

Copyright © 2023 Warren H. Lau.

ISBN: 979-8215595107

Written by Warren H. Lau.

Table of Contents

To Everyone Who Has a Computer and/or Smart Device

Your System's Sweetspots
CEO's Advice on Basic Cyber Security

Preface - The Best Way to Protect Your System is to Think Like a Hacker

One of the best things you can do in business is to pre-test the security of all your interacting objects - websites, mobile applications, networks, etc. Complying with the law is just as important as protecting your systems and networks from criminal hacker attacks.

Ethical hackers and penetration testers can secure potential entry points, make sure all systems and applications are password protected, and secure network infrastructure with a firewall. Experienced hackers can often break into a system with complex lines of code to steal data, cause damage, or provide the hacker with an alternative entry point. An attacker can use various tools and methods to gain access and gain access to the system. The next step in hacking is when an attacker uses every means to gain unauthorized access to targeted systems, applications, or networks.

During the scan, the hacker continuously uses the target system, launches DDoS attacks, uses the captured system as a springboard, or steals the entire database. Ethical hackers or penetration testers can use scanning to scan an organization's entire infrastructure for malicious activity and find the root cause to prevent systems from being exploited. The purpose of this step is to test whether the target's vulnerabilities can be exploited to gain a permanent presence on the production system long enough for an attacker to gain deep access.

Testers then try to exploit these vulnerabilities—usually through privilege escalation, data theft, traffic eavesdropping, and so on—to see what damage they can cause. Attack vectors allow hackers to exploit system vulnerabilities, including human error. Often, red hat hackers deploy cyberattacks on intruder systems.

White hat hackers, commonly known as ethical hackers, are often hired by companies and government agencies to test security vulnerabilities. They apply cybersecurity techniques, commonly known as penetration testing and deep vulnerability assessments, to make sure security systems work. Many professional hackers use their skills to identify security holes in corporate systems and then advise where companies need to beef up their defenses to keep attackers out.

Hackers can also use their technical skills to install malware, steal or destroy data, or disrupt an organization's services. Not only do hackers break into businesses and demand ransom, but they also try to break into ordinary user accounts and try to take advantage of things like online banking, online trading, etc. Hackers can infiltrate a company's website, steal data (cross-scripting) and/or use them to distribute malware and viruses to unsuspecting visitors.

If malware lands on any of your connected devices, it can spread to other devices connected to your home network. As a result, the number of cybersecurity attacks that use the network to access corporate devices is huge and scary.

Your devices, accounts, and your entire network are as secure as your router. You can check the security of your home network, but you cannot do the same for a public Wi-Fi network. Keep your network access and your personal data secure and don't leave windows or doors open for a hacker to access. You don't want to leave the door open for hackers to get your information.

When scammers, hackers, and other intruders try to steal your personal information online, it can be helpful to know how to lock down your device, network, and information. These tips should help you prevent hackers from violating your personal security on your computer and other devices. Protect your computer and other devices with antivirus and antimalware software.

Keep your security software, internet browser and operating system up to date. For information on how to update your security software, operating system, internet browsers, and apps, visit the developer's website. While no one is immune from a data breach, good cybersecurity habits can make you less vulnerable and help you survive a data breach with fewer disruptions.

To keep up with the bad guys, you need to first understand your vulnerabilities, understand the many ways your defenses can be compromised, and then implement the defenses you need to maintain a safe and resilient cybersecurity posture. The consequences of a lack of effective cybersecurity can be catastrophic.

Devices and users that connect to unsecured networks and applications are at risk and may even be compromised. Mobile devices can act as a secondary means of protecting your online accounts through 2FA, but these endpoints can also be a weak link, completely compromising your privacy and security. A vulnerability in mobile devices is a vulnerability that could allow an attacker to lower the security of systems. This can leave many devices vulnerable, allowing attackers in some cases to take over your IoT devices for further attacks, or even spy on your company that the cameras are connected to.

You are less likely to be hacked with an exploit, but many computer users have been affected by malware downloaded as part of a software package or injected into their computer via a phishing attack. In the examples of security breaches above, several methods were used to gain access to networks: Yahoo was phished, and Facebook was hacked with an exploit.

Attackers can also target their malware across multiple platforms and potentially find malware that attacks one operating system but is able to spread to others. In spear phishing attacks, attackers target potential victims with deep knowledge of them, a method that allows them to customize their attacks. The type of information these criminals are looking for can vary, but when individuals are targeted, criminals often try to trick you into giving them passwords or banking information, or install stealthy malware on your computer that allows They are able to access. your passwords and banking information and let them control your computer.

Introduction to Your System's Sweetspots

Computer Systems Nowadays have become more sophisticated, more convenient to use, however, the convenience comes in a price. The system nowadays are more vulnerable to cyber attacks!

What to do if your computer/ smartphone/ website server is compromised?

What to do if your email account is PWNed?

Or, if your friends, relatives or employers face the above problem, what would you do to help them?

In this book, you will learn about the most recent hackers tricks, most prevalent form of cyberattacks that personal computers and website managers nowadays have to deal with.

Introduction to CEO's Advice on Computer Science

Let's face it. The traditional schooling system's focus on computer science is severely inadequate. In order to survive an ever developing computer driven world, in order to equip yourselves or your children with sufficient computer knowledge, so to have better employment or better living standards, the smart choice will be to seek new solutions from experts who have already spent decades in this field.

And that is why the cyber education series, "CEO's Advice on Computer Science", is published for you.

In this series, we would discuss the most sought after topics in Computer Science, including SEO, ASO, Cybersecurity, Computer Programming, Coding Skills, eCommerce, and other useful techniques that you would find very useful in your future career path, whether you wish to seek a job in large companies or tech firms, or even though you wish to run your own startup.

Part One: Cyber Security for Personal Computers

Make Use of Windows Defender Wisely

Windows 10 includes Windows Security, which provides the latest virus protection. Although Microsoft no longer offers security updates for Windows 7, Avast continues to protect its users with the Windows 7 version, making Avast Free Antivirus one of the best antivirus solutions for Windows 10 and Windows 7. In addition, we keep Avast Free Antivirus updated all the time. to make sure you stay protected no matter what threats arise. With the free Microsoft Defender Antivirus software running on Windows 10 Windows 10, you have the security of protecting against malware should you let your guard down.

Detecting threats with Microsoft Defender should be the starting point for better antivirus security on Windows, and most people will find it unnecessary to go any further when deciding on an antivirus solution. I spent weeks testing Microsoft Windows Defender and all the best antivirus software on the market, ranking them based on malware detection rate, system performance, scan speed, overall internet security protection, and customer support. We set out to create the standard Wirecutter guide for the best antivirus apps, so we spent months researching the software, reading reports from independent testing labs and agencies, and consulting with cybersecurity experts. If you're not sure which of the many antivirus utilities available is right for you, we can help.

If you're still not convinced that none of the above products provide Microsoft with the best free antivirus software, the solutions below are still strong players against all types of malware, not just viruses. These commercial products offer protection beyond Windows 10's built-in antivirus; the best free antivirus utilities offer more than Windows offers. Again, there are better free Microsoft antivirus software out there, and no free antivirus software offers the kind of protection you get with full premium antivirus software. In fact, you can get high-quality protection completely free these days, as almost every major vendor offers free antivirus software.

AVG AntiVirus FREE now also offers best-in-class ransomware protection, previously only available as a premium feature. Best of all, the malware protection in Kaspersky Security Cloud Free Antivirus is a snapshot from Kasperskys or Bitdefenders, whose free programs bother us less with paid updates and load less on the system. We still recommend Kaspersky Security Cloud Free, it has less impact on the system, better protection against malware, and more useful plugins, but there is absolutely nothing wrong with using Microsoft's built-in antivirus as your antivirus solution. Windows Defender itself won't have many extra features, but Windows 10 does have parental controls, a gaming mode, and protection for Windows 10 Edge and Internet Explorer browsers.

Norton 360 is the best Microsoft security package on the market. Norton 360 offers significant improvements to all of Microsoft's Windows Defender protections and offers many additional features that Microsoft doesn't include in its built-in antivirus software. Best of all, Norton 360 offers a range of Windows antivirus packages to suit every budget, all of which include free features like VPNs and password managers. This premium software offers everything you need, such as fraud protection, virus protection, built-in VPN, and more. Sophos Home Antivirus offers virus and malware protection as well as phishing protection and even content control, which is also ideal for parents.

This free antivirus program is built into Windows and enabled by default, so just turn it on and this antivirus solution will cover the basics of internet security. An excellent corporate antivirus package that offers various tools such as antivirus protection, firewall, email protection, spam protection and the ability to isolate applications for complete security. Avira Antivirus Free Avira is one of the best free antivirus solutions. In addition to protecting your Windows 10 PC, you can also add protection for your phone. With a single subscription to McAfee AntiVirus Plus, you can protect all your Windows, Android, Mac OS, and iOS devices.

Depending on the level you choose, Microsoft Defender Antivirus can protect both Windows 10 and Mac, as well as mobile devices with five secure devices and a built-in password manager. Upgrade to Trend Micro's full security and you can count on Mac and mobile protection, as well as Windows, covering a total of 10 devices. In any case, you have enough time to test Aviras Free Security Suite and decide if this antivirus is suitable for protecting your Windows device. Other Windows programs include Avira Free Security Suite, Avira Antivirus Pro, Bitdefender Antivirus Free Edition, and Bitdefender Internet Security.

This list does not include Windows Phone 7 and Windows Phone 8 because they do not support running security software. The best antivirus vendors usually offer more paid Windows products that have the same malware protection but with additional features as prices rise. You have the option to use Bitdefender as a standalone antivirus, or use many of Bitdefender's features in conjunction with Microsoft Defender. Many users are reluctant to switch to a third-party antivirus because they think it will be more difficult than Microsoft Windows Defender Auto-Protect, but Bitdefender is actually even more practical than Defender.

Microsoft Defender's number one with a powerful antivirus engine, Windows-specific security features, firewall, VPN and more. Bitdefender Total Security 2020 allows you to protect five devices (Windows, MacOS, iOS, and Android), set up parental controls on a child's computer, and run a VPN. Sometimes it's nice to know that antivirus vendors are doing the right thing by constantly updating their Internet security software packages to protect you from ever-increasing threats to your online life.

Firewall Settings for Windows

I will give some tips to help illustrate the process so you can understand how to set up a firewall in 5 steps. When using the guides, or even if you decide to set up your firewall, make sure you have a security expert review your configuration to make sure it's set up to keep your data as secure as possible. Setting up a firewall can be an intimidating project, but breaking down work into simpler tasks can make the job much more manageable.

If you are already using a firewall to prevent cyberattacks, perhaps more information on how it works will improve your ability to manage a firewall with more personalization at home and in the office. Using a firewall is also important to protect data from malicious attacks. Firewalls provide protection against external cyber attacks by protecting your computer or network from malicious or unnecessary network traffic.

Firewalls can be configured to block data from specific locations (such as computer network addresses), applications, or ports, allowing important and necessary data to pass through. Firewalls also prevent malicious software from accessing a computer or network over the Internet. Firewalls filter incoming and in some cases outgoing traffic by comparing packets against predefined rules and policies, preventing threats from entering the network.

Firewalls prevent unauthorized access to the corporate network and warns of any intrusion attempts. Hardware firewalls are especially useful for protecting multiple computers and controlling network activity trying to pass through them. Host firewalls are also useful for homes where multiple computers share the same network. A host firewall is also recommended for corporate computers that are connected to the network but are not protected by a network firewall.

If you have a larger business, you can purchase an optional corporate network firewall. You can also buy a hardware firewall from companies like Cisco, Sophos, or Fortinet, depending on your broadband router, which also has a built-in firewall to protect your network. Your router should also have a built-in firewall to prevent attacks on your network. There are many suitable firewall models you can use to protect your network.

Configuring Windows Firewall according to the following guidelines will help you optimize the protection of devices on your network. You can protect your computer by using firewall and antivirus software and by following computer usage guidelines. Combining a firewall with other security measures such as antivirus software and secure processing technology will increase your resistance to attacks. Antivirus software, antispyware software, and firewalls are also important tools for preventing devices from being attacked.

By using security measures and best practices to protect your device, you can protect your privacy and your family. You can protect your mobile device by turning off Bluetooth when not in use, keeping an eye on the Wi-Fi networks you're connected to, and using security apps to improve monitoring and protection. Implementing mobile device security measures restricts device access to the network, a necessary step to ensure that network traffic remains private and cannot escape through vulnerable mobile connections. Mobile devices can act as an aid to securing your online accounts with 2FA, but these endpoints can also be a weak link that completely compromises your privacy and security.

Using security policies, you can restrict network access to authorized users and devices only, or restrict access to incompatible devices or guest users. When designing a set of firewall policies for your network, it is recommended that you set authorization rules for any network applications deployed on hosts. These settings are designed to protect the device from use in most network scenarios. The overview panel shows the security settings for each type of network the device can connect to.

Firewall protection is the first and most important configuration step. As the first line of defense against online attacks, a firewall is a key part of network security. If an attacker can gain administrative access to your firewall, it means it's game over for your network's security.

Even if hackers know where your computer is, the firewall is holding them back. The firewall prevents hackers from seeing your computer on the network while looking for victims. You can restrict external access to your computer and information on it using a firewall. A firewall helps keep hackers, viruses, and other malicious activity out of the Internet and determines what traffic can enter your device.

YOUR SYSTEM'S SWEETSPOTS: CEO'S ADVICE ON BASIC CYBER SECURITY

Turn on a firewall for more security on devices, or use a virtual private network (VPN), especially when accessing resources remotely. Network security with MFA and protect sensitive data such as your email network and critical CRM infrastructure.

Using a secure password is the most important way to prevent network intrusions. Using strong passwords and advanced authentication methods helps protect your personal information. If you have too many passwords to remember, consider using password management software that can help you create strong personal passwords and keep them safe.

When setting up a network, log into your router and set a password using a secure, encrypted setting. More effective authentication methods may include the use of a fingerprint, one-time codes sent to a mobile device, or other features that provide user access to an account.

Windows and Mac have nice built-in firewalls, and many third-party security programs include them. A properly configured firewall can effectively block some attacks, don't let yourself fall into a false sense of security.

If your firewall can also act as a Dynamic Host Configuration Protocol (DHCP) server, Network Time Protocol (NTP) server, Intrusion Prevention System (IPS), etc., configure the services you want to use. This assumes that you are using an enterprise-class firewall that supports multiple internal networks (or zones) and performs stateful packet inspection.

Do Not Keep Your Browsing Histories and Cookies

Clear your browsing history frequently, including cookies and cached files, to give hackers as little information as possible to work with if your phone is compromised. However, cyberattacks can steal cookies and access your browsing history. Hackers can intercept information collected through cookies because there is no protection to prevent access. Third parties can steal cookies by copying unencrypted session data and using it to impersonate the user.

With all of this data collected, companies may use cookies to their advantage, and in some cases, to your advantage. The cookies can then track and collect data from your browser, sending this information to the website owner.

Web browsers read and write Flash cookies and can track any data while using the web. Cookies are stored in your device's web browser if you accept them. GDPR law requires all multinational companies to grant permission, under which website owners obtain the user's permission to use cookies before they can be stored in the user's web browser cookies.

Legitimate websites use cookies to offer regular users special offers and track the effectiveness of their ads. Some online platforms are vulnerable to hackers who steal cookies, which can lead to identity theft. Click Manage Website Data to see which websites have trackers and cookies idle in your browser.

When you visit various websites, many of them store data on your hard drive about your visit, called "cookies". You can view all cookie data by looking at the settings area of some web browsers. Cookies may also track your preferences in order to show them websites that may be of interest to them.

You can also set your preferences so that websites do not store cookies. In the same three-dot menu as in a Browser, you can also block third-party cookies by selecting "Settings", then scrolling to the "Privacy and Security" section and clicking "Cookies and other site data". Generally, you can change your settings to limit the use of cookies and improve your privacy. Cookies can be useful, not only invasive, but for greater privacy, you can block them completely: both the website publisher's own cookies and third-party cookies from others, such as advertisers.

To understand why cookies can be useful, it's important to understand what data cookies can store about you. It depends on who will have access to your data and what they will do with it, and also on the fact that the rejection of cookies will affect your ability to use the website you are visiting.

A web server can use cookies to customize the display it sends to the user, or it can track the individual pages of the website that the user visits. HTTP cookies can also be used to track users by storing special usage history data in cookies, such as those used by Google Analytics, called tracking cookies. HTTP cookies are data stored on a user's computer to facilitate automated access to a website or other state information required for web functionality or complex websites.

Cookies are information sent by a web server to a user's browser. Cookies are small text files sent from the website you are visiting to the computer or device you are using. Cookies were developed as a reliable mechanism for websites to remember information or record the browsing history of users. Cookies, those bits of data that are stored in your browser that allow websites to track user information, allow you to stay logged into your online account when you open your browser.

Cookies stored in your web browser may also remember your login credentials. Cookies can be useful as they save you time, for example when entering login details for a previously visited website.

Cookies can be used to store login information, credit card information, and to help advertisers deliver ads they think match your preferences. Your browsing data includes cookies, ISP logs and browser plug-ins that may store data. While consumers have little protection against ISP-level attacks, the web pages they visit can also be tracked using cookies, which are small pieces of text downloaded and stored by the browser.

Many ISPs share this information with advertising agencies, who in turn will use the information to show you relevant ads. Become has been challenged by privacy groups as companies like Google collect massive amounts of consumer data to serve personalized ads based on browser history. Cookies are used to personalize your browsing experience and this may include tailored advertising.

With some caveats, private browsing will protect your privacy from other people using your computer and will reduce some of the information you reveal about yourself when you visit websites. Calling your browsing data anti-hacker software might be a step too far - it won't stop a determined hacker, but using such software can make it harder for a hacker to break into your computer or access your data.

In Internet Explorer, a file known as index.dat is stored on the system, which is also responsible for storing information about cookies and browsing history. In one case, index.dat is used by the operating system to store a list of previously visited websites, and another index.dat elsewhere is used to store cookie information on the system. Internet Explorer offers the option to delete index.dat and clear the cache of index.dat files and web pages, but using both cannot be completely cleared, meaning the content will always be cached on disk no matter what the user does. can experience.

If you are using the Firefox browser, there is an add-on called Better Privacy that can help you remove Flash cookies. The normal procedures for clearing standard cookies, clearing history, clearing the cache, or selecting the clear personal data option in the browser will not affect Flash cookies.

A way to start a Windows computer that can help you diagnose problems; access is granted only to essential files and drivers. A set of specifications that enables a computer to automatically detect and configure devices and install appropriate device drivers.

Media Access Control; the hardware address of the device connected to the public network. A DMR is a hardware device connected to a wired or wireless network that you can control using a computer. Internet Connection Sharing; a Windows feature that, when enabled, allows you to connect your home network computer to the Internet through your computer.

The process of entering a username and password to log into a specific computer; for example, a mainframe, a secure network, or a server, or other system that can share resources. Authentication system developed at the Massachusetts Institute of Technology (MIT); allows the exchange of private information over an open network by assigning a unique key, called a "ticket", to the user who requests access to protect the information. One use of the term "cybersecurity" refers to the technology used to implement secure operating systems.

Access control systems provide computer security and can also be used to control access to secured buildings. User account access control and encryption can protect system files and data, respectively. The TOSHIBA Password Utility allows you to set up and maintain password protection that restricts access to your computer. The TOSHIBA Security Assist utility acts as a ``command center" where you can set various passwords or other security features and see how these features can be used with each other to further enhance the security or simplify the protection of your system.

TOSHIBA Assist provides quick access to computer features and allows you to configure various computer settings. The TOSHIBA system settings will open, allowing you to configure certain settings on your computer.

You can change your previously saved site settings without going to the Site Settings menu in Chrome. Scroll down to the "Privacy and Security" section and select "Site Settings" from the menu. You can set site permissions without changing the default settings. Access controls include location, camera, microphone, notifications, and audio, which determine whether a site can start playing audio without your permission. To quickly return all of these settings to their default state, click Reset Permissions.

If you enable this option, sites may request permission to access the microphone, and you can allow or block them depending on your needs. You can also allow or block the camera and microphone in the Android Chrome browser. Many applications and services require and use a camera or microphone, and Windows settings allow you to control which applications can use the camera or microphone.

The Google Chrome camera settings along with the microphone access settings is one of the best features offered by Google Chrome. On Windows, having a camera and microphone on your device lets you make video calls in Teams, take photos, record videos, and more. Learn how to disable camera and microphone access and website permissions on your google chrome google chrome computer.

Therefore, when using online banking, you need to ensure that you use a secure verification method, such as only using the respective bank's app, and never enter your login details in the web interface. If you're connecting to a public Wi-Fi hotspot, one of the most important layers of security to implement is to use a virtual private network (VPN), and a reliable VPN must be implemented on all devices, regardless of your device. good connection.

YOUR SYSTEM'S SWEETSPOTS: CEO'S ADVICE ON BASIC CYBER SECURITY

Due to the need for compromised physical access (or sophisticated backdoors), devices and methods such as dongles, TPMs, anti-intrusion enclosures, drive locks, USB disabling, and mobile access can be considered more secure. A Trusted Platform Module (TPM) protects a device by integrating cryptographic functions into an access device using a microprocessor or so-called computer-on-chip. They can also compromise security by changing the operating system, installing software worms, keyloggers, hidden listening devices, or using wireless microphones. Devices that have been compromised by malware can infiltrate your network, people can drop malware on systems themselves, and some malware sits idle waiting to be attacked.

Reading passwords, logging keystrokes, or opening doors for new malware, or even hijacking your entire computer, it all goes crazy. The Trojan named Skygofree has extremely advanced features, such as the ability to connect to Wi-Fi networks on its own even if the user has disabled this feature on their device. This type of Trojan can change data on your computer, crash your computer or make certain data unavailable to you.

If you have set system restore points in Windows when malware attacks and cannot be fixed, take this opportunity to restore your system. To reboot, go to Settings > Update & Security > Windows Security > Virus & Threat Protection. Or do a real ``nuclear" option of reformatting the hard drive and reinstalling the OS and all programs (you have a Windows 10 clean install backup image that you can use to restore, right?).

To do this, open Settings > Security & Location/Security > Find My Device. If you have such a device, you can usually encrypt your smartphone via Settings > Security > Encrypt device. The device can be read in its entirety, calls can be recorded, or the phone can be used as a listening device.

Internet Browser Security Settings

If you choose to use Edge, the first thing you need to do is customize your browser, including changing all settings to suit your needs. As you'll see, Edge now supports default settings that users can override, as well as mandatory settings (users can't override). On the General Settings page, change the value in the Configured section to include settings in this policy. Configure the settings you want for your environment, such as the home page URL, security settings, and so on.

The Settings menu will now display settings related to privacy and security. Now click on the "Privacy, search and services" tab in the left sidebar and right pane, scroll down and you will see the "Enable Security Measures" option for a more secure browsing experience. The description of the setting says: "Turn on this mode for safer web browsing and protection of your browser from malware. You can now enable/disable Super Duper Secure mode using the Microsoft Edge web browser settings page as described in the method mentioned above.

In the latest version of Edge Canary Edge Canary, Microsoft has added a new flag that allows you to enable "Super Duper Protected Mode" with a dedicated toggle in the "Super Duper Protected Mode" settings - a dedicated switch in Settings. Super Duper Secure Mode is a special feature developed by the Microsoft Edge web browser team that can be used by Edge users to improve security and provide a secure browsing experience. In their quest to create something that can change the modern exploit landscape and significantly increase the cost of exploits for attackers, Microsoft has launched Super Duper Secure mode in Edge Edge. Microsoft says "Super-Duper Secure Mode" is just another experiment, so Microsoft isn't 100% sure it's coming to Edge Stable.

In addition to prevention, the Edge browser will use the following advanced security features to keep you safe while browsing the web. This Edge setting will block trackers on all websites, reduce personalization, and block other malicious trackers. To continue with the wizard, be sure to configure the "Set Edge browser as default" option.

If you want to switch back to using the Chromium engine, simply open Edge Settings and another menu again and select Exit Internet Explorer Mode. Find the "Internet Explorer (IE) Compatibility" section on the right side of the settings page.

If you'd rather use a different search engine for your searches and suggestions, go to Edge Settings > Privacy & Services. How to find out, read our post about changing the search engine used in Edge.

If you want to clear all saved passwords for the current profile, use the Clear browsing data option on the Privacy and Services page in Edge settings. There, you can activate or deactivate the password manager using the "Suggestions for saved passwords" option; the second switch allows you to configure whether the new Edge browser will allow you to log in automatically with saved passwords. As mentioned above, you need to use a dedicated password manager instead of relying on Edge (or even any browser), so disable this recommendation.

Note that you can configure most of the new Edge browser options that I describe here by clicking the three dots in the top right corner of the browser window (or pressing Alt + F) and then selecting Preferences from the Edge menu. When you open a new tab (by pressing Ctrl+T or by clicking the plus sign to the right of the current tab group), Edge displays a default page that aggressively links to Microsoft services. When you sign in to the new Edge browser with an Azure AD account associated with an Office 365 Business or Enterprise subscription, you can replace Microsoft News content with links to Office 365 documents and services, but the fourth option isn't available.

In the advanced settings menu, you can also choose how Microsoft Edge handles cookies (you can choose to block all cookies, block only third-party cookies, or don't block cookies) and save form data/passwords. If you've implemented Microsoft Intune for MDM and manage Windows 10 only with Intune or with co-management with configuration management, you can configure Edge settings with Intune. For clients using the legacy Microsoft Edge web browser on Windows 10 clients, create a Microsoft Endpoint Configuration Manager compliance policy to configure browser settings. If you only want to deploy perimeter security settings, you can stick with the Microsoft Perimeter Security Baselines, but if you want to deploy some advanced settings as well, I recommend creating a new Settings Catalog or Administrative Template.

Disabling Password Save Prompts If you've saved passwords, or if Web Browser is set to require you to save passwords every time you enter your credentials on a website, you'll see something similar to the image below. This post shows you how to disable password hints for saving credentials, as well as hints for saving credit card payment methods in Web Browser.

Saving a password in Browser for your credentials is enabled by default, but you can disable this option. Saved passwords. Select this option to import your online account credentials saved in Browser into the new Microsoft Edge so you can sign in to your online accounts quickly and securely.

When you sign in to the Google Web Browser with your Google Account, Web Browser may offer to save your passwords, payment methods, and related information to your Google Account. If you use a payment method from your Google Account or choose to save a payment method to your Google Account for future use, Web Browser will collect information on your computer and pass it to Google Pay to protect you from fraud and provide the service. While this policy describes certain features of the Google Web Browser, any personal information provided by Google or stored in your Google account will be used and protected in accordance with the Google Privacy Policy, as amended from time to time. Personal information stored in Web Browser will not be sent to Google unless you choose to store this data in your Google account by activating sync or, in the case of passwords, payment cards and payment information, selecting specific credentials or a payment card and billing information to be stored in your Google account.

You can let Web Browser remember passwords for websites and automatically sign you in using passwords saved in your Google account. The next time you open this website, Web Browser will automatically enter your credentials. This way, the next time you visit a website or service, the password manager will automatically fill in the forms with your saved login information. You can automatically enter a secure password on new accounts or directly on the login page.

A password manager is essentially an encrypted digital vault that stores password-protected, secure login information that you can use to log into applications and accounts on mobile devices, websites, and other services. Plus, store your passwords in a centralized password manager that you can use across all browsers and devices. Our best password management options also include subscription options that let you sync secure password login details across devices, share credentials with trusted family and friends, and access secure online storage. If you use multiple devices, you want the manager to be available on all your devices and all browsers so that you can access your passwords and logins, including credit cards, from anywhere through the manager app or its browser extensions and shipping information.

You can of course use Web Browser, Safari or Firefox to manage your passwords, addresses and other login details. While using an online browser password tool is certainly better than not using a password manager at all, you can't easily access your passwords and other logins outside your browser, or share your logins with others you trust. Many times, if one account is hacked, your data is no longer safe in other accounts that use the same login information, especially if you use the same password for multiple services. If you use the same password for multiple accounts, someone who steals your password will have access to all of your accounts, not just one.

If you use a password for authentication only, anyone who knows this password owns your account. Anyone who receives your password can log into your account and make purchases without your knowledge or receive your personal information. Using it ensures that if someone decrypts your account password, they can't log in unless they can log into your account unless they also get access to your code, which means they must also own your mobile device. The single best way to prevent the domino effect of a data breach is to use a strong unique password for each of your online accounts.

Given the number of password-protected accounts you have, it's unlikely that you'll remember all of your strong passwords. When using multiple online services, it can be difficult to remember complex password credentials, and this is where password vaults come into play. When you register on the website, you may be asked to create security questions and answers to verify your identity if your password is lost. You basically use multiple passwords to create your own security features.

Create different passwords for each website account, your computer and wireless network. You can even set a master password to unlock your browser credentials. To view passwords saved in Internet Explorer, select Tools > Internet Options > Content tab > AutoFill Options > Manage Passwords.

Here, you'll find all the passwords Browser has saved for you, as well as a "suggested" option for saving passwords. For verification purposes, when you enter a website, Browser sends a partial hash of your username and other encrypted information about your password to Google, which then returns a list. If you're a user of Google services, you can use your privacy controls to prevent Google from storing your search results, YouTube history, device information, and use your data to determine whether you're happy with Google's customization of ads.

The Built-in Remote Access Function of Windows

To use a remote desktop session, the user or administrator must use RDP client software to connect to the remote PC or Windows server where the RDP server software is to be run. The other computer must be running RDP server software that allows clients to connect remotely. To allow remote connections, the other computer must be running Windows 10 Pro or Enterprise.

Once the connection is established, the user can remotely log in to another computer. Once connected, the user who submitted the RDP connection request will be able to see the desktop of the computer they are connecting to via RDP.

During the lifetime of an RDP connection, the client and the remote server exchange basic input/output data. Communication during an RDP connection will be highly asymmetric, with most of the data being sent from the remote server to the client. After the RDP connection is completed, most of the data sent between the client and server will consist of input data (client->server) and graphics data (server->client). The connection is acknowledged by the remote server using an X.224 connection handshake PDU.

RDP establishes a dedicated encrypted network connection between a host system and a remote host system device. RDP is a secure network communication protocol created by Microsoft that provides remote access to applications and desktops. Because RDP is part of Microsoft's server and desktop operating systems, it's easy to implement as a remote access solution. In addition to being used to access remote computers, Microsoft uses the RDP cloud computing solution on Microsoft Azure to serve virtual machines for users.

RDP also supports numerous Windows operating systems and devices, providing strong physical security through remote data storage. The RDP server is integrated into the Microsoft operating system and can be enabled through the Server Manager panel. RDP Features and Functions RDP is a secure and interoperable protocol that creates secure connections between clients, servers, and virtual machines.

While the latest version of Remote Desktop (RDP) offers greatly improved security protocols, it is recommended that you use both RDP and VPN, as this combination provides the highest security when accessing computers and servers remotely. It is strongly recommended to use an RDP gateway to restrict RDP access to desktops and servers (see discussion below). This means that RDP helps protect remote connections from many data security threats.

The RDP protocol provides remote access over a dedicated network channel. RDP provides a graphical interface for remotely connecting one computer to another. RDP works by broadcasting an output device, such as a monitor, from a remote computer to a client computer.

The client machine's input devices (eg, mouse and keyboard) are transferred to the remote computer. VNC works on a server/client model, and as soon as the server (the local computer accessed remotely) and the viewer (the user accessing the local computer remotely) connect, the server sends a copy of the remote desktop screen to the remote viewer.

VNC connects to the user's RDP session, but cannot be used to create virtual desktops. RDP gives users access to these virtual desktops whether they are in the office or working remotely. Essentially, RDP allows users to manage their remote Windows machines as if they were working locally (well, almost).

For example, if you want to access your PC from a laptop or other device, you can use RDP to connect to the remote PC, view content on the remote monitor, and interact as if you were working locally on that computer. As long as another machine is turned on and configured to connect remotely, you can get files, open applications, fix problems, or just work remotely. Often, you can use a modern legacy Remote Desktop or Remote Desktop Connection application to provide assistance or control a computer or server without physically visiting the location. Windows Remote Desktop Control is also disabled by default, so you need to enable it before you can use it to make Remote Desktop connections in Windows 10.

If you're in a clean Windows environment, here's how to enable the Remote Desktop application, which lets you connect to a Windows computer remotely. Although you can use the Control Panel to set up Remote Desktop in Windows 10 and earlier (such as Windows 8.1 and Windows 7), the ability to enable Remote Desktop using the Settings app is only available starting with Windows 10 Fall Creators Update and later . Version. Right-click the "PC" icon on the desktop, select "Properties" from the drop-down list, and then select "Remote Settings" from the list on the left.

Network administrators use RDP to diagnose problems, log in to servers, and perform other remote operations. Remote workers use RDP to access an organization's network to access email and files. RDP is a Microsoft proprietary protocol that allows you to connect to other computers remotely, usually over TCP port 3389. Client computers initiate communication with the host using an RDP server, which provides a GUI over a network connection, and the teleworker service software is software that runs over the RDP protocol.

We now have a hung pointer, and the next time the remote server tries to access the MS_T120 channel (which is often the case, since the MS_T120 channel is an important channel for RDP to work), the system will check for errors.

Shared Experience Settings

Customize Windows Defender Antivirus to quickly detect and prevent threats using native resources and machine learning. Learn how to use your profile to customize these settings. To use the exploit protection settings in this profile, you must create an XML configuration file using the Windows Security app or PowerShell on the same device before creating the profile.

In addition to configuration profiles, native Windows scripts are used to deploy a configuration when there is no natively supported configuration item to configure a setting on a Windows device. This includes specific configuration for Windows devices for antivirus, drive encryption, firewall, endpoint detection and response, attack surface mitigation, account protection, and Microsoft Defender for endpoints. This includes macro security, Windows 10 Enhanced Security (ACSC), Windows Hello, Admin Lockout, Deployment Optimization, disable Adobe Flash, Microsoft Store, Defender, Network Border, OneDrive, Time Zone, Bitlocker, and Windows 10 Enterprise settings. Workspace ONE UEM uses these settings to protect Windows devices from exploits, reduce attack surfaces, control folder access, and secure network connections.

Use a user settings profile to prevent end users from turning off the airwatch service on their Windows devices. Select the Use recommended Windows settings check box to use the recommended Windows settings and disable all other settings available in the encryption profile.

For example, if Controlled Folder Access is set to Enabled, Windows Defender will use the vulnerability to block access to protected folders. You can also enable the Protected Folders option in the same settings area to protect individual folders and files.

This policy setting controls user attempts to access file system objects on removable storage devices. On Windows 10, you can configure this policy setting to determine the level of diagnostic data to send to Windows. You can stop sending this data to Microsoft and stop collecting it entirely by checking the box at the top of the Privacy Options page.

If you have more than one eligible phone, you will need to select one. If your phone qualifies, Google will automatically use the security key built into your phone for added security when you sign in to new devices. You can set up your phone's built-in security key for secure sign-in on Web Browser OS, iOS, macOS, and Windows 10 devices. To set up your phone's built-in security key, you need a phone running Android 7.0 or later.

With a few control panel tweaks and other methods, you can make sure you have all the necessary security tools set up to protect your operating system. You can protect your computer with firewall and antivirus software and by following best computer practices. Antivirus programs such as Bitdefender, Panda Free Antivirus, Malwarebytes, and Avast protect your computer from unauthorized code or programs that could threaten your operating system. You can use tools built into Windows 10 to prevent viruses and malicious code.

Microsoft provides many exploit protections that are built into the operating system and do not require configuration on the operating system. Microsoft's custom protections designed to protect against memory manipulation require a deep understanding of these threats and remedies, as well as an understanding of how the operating system and applications manage memory.

Windows 10 uses protected processes more widely in the operating system and, like Windows 8.1, implements protected processes in a way that third-party antimalware vendors can use, as described in Protecting Antimalware Services.

The Enterprise edition of Windows 10 includes Windows Defender Advanced Threat Protection, a security platform that uses behavioral sensors to monitor endpoints like Windows 10 PCs. Most devices use firewalls or closely related tools to inspect traffic and eliminate threats. Firewalls are used in personal and corporate settings, and many devices come with built-in ones, including Mac, Windows, and Linux computers. Hardware/firmware firewalls are often used to set restrictions between devices in the home.

Firewalls must be configured to restrict access via software or hardware or both. Firewalls can be the first line of defense in network security by limiting who can access remotely. Organizations can use an internal firewall on the perimeter firewall to segment the network and provide internal protection.

There are several ways to protect your computer, network, files and data when using remote access. It is helpful to understand how remote computer access works, possible security risks, and how to securely access other computers and networks remotely. This describes how to use antivirus tools, disable automatic login, disable remote login, set up encryption, and more.

To generate Microsoft mitigation policies from an EMET settings XML file, you can install the ProcessMitigations PowerShell module. Hardening your Windows 10 PC means you're adjusting your security settings. If you're concerned about the privacy of your data, you don't want to leave the default settings on your devices, including everything running Windows 10.

Check these privacy options as soon as you set up your Windows 10 PC, or now if you're a longtime user who hasn't been able to do so yet. When connecting to a new Wi-Fi hotspot on Microsoft Windows computers, be sure to select "Public" when the option appears, as this will allow the operating system to disable sharing; Turn off your Wi-Fi connection when you don't need it, turn on firewalls, and try to only visit websites with HTTPS enabled. Network Protection prevents users from using any application to access dangerous domains that could host phishing, exploit, or malware attacks.

Windows Defender, configured for all your devices, keeps end users safe while using the device. Application layer firewall rules can also be used to control the execution of files or the processing of data by specific applications. Credential Guard also includes a powerful system protector called Hypervisor Protected Code Integrity (HVCI), which uses virtualization-based security (VBS) to protect Microsoft's Kernel-Mode Code Integrity check process.

Blue Tooth Settings

This is to prevent hackers from discovering your Bluetooth device, as long as you make it discoverable during pairing. By using this strategy, you have more control over the discoverability of your Bluetooth device, because you don't need to make the Bluetooth device discoverable to connect to a new headset after the initial pairing. Even with Bluetooth discovery disabled, previously paired devices are still able to connect to the computer. After a few times, the risk of an intruder getting close and hacking your device via Bluetooth decreases.

Hackers deliberately look for a Bluetooth security hole; once they find it, they use it to gain access to devices and information they shouldn't. Hackers use a variety of methods to break into Bluetooth-enabled devices, and new vulnerabilities are discovered regularly. Here are some ways to protect yourself from hackers trying to gain access to your Bluetooth device.

Wi-Fi networks and Bluetooth connections can be vulnerable access points for data or identity theft. Like Wi-Fi, hackers use Bluetooth to break into your device and steal your identity. Like Wi-Fi connections, Bluetooth can put your personal data at risk if you're not careful.

Some Bluetooth features act like an attractive hassle that puts your device and data at risk and doesn't require hacking. Bluetooth Security Bluetooth Security The Bluetooth connection to your mobile device can be used to connect wireless headphones, transfer files, turn on speakers while driving, and more. Bluetooth is a technology that allows electronic devices such as smartphones, tablets, portable speakers, digital assistants, wearable fitness trackers and home security devices to connect wirelessly with each other. Using the "power" of this technology, Bluetooth hackers can easily compromise the online security of any unsecured device.

With this form of Bluetooth attack, hackers can also take full control of your device. During bluebugging, experienced hackers can gain full access and control over the device. Bluebugging is the most dangerous threat to Bluetooth devices because it gives hackers complete control over the device and its movement commands. Some cybercriminals have even found a way to hack into a device's Bluetooth connection and take control of it - in just 10 seconds.

If hackers can replicate a trusted network, they can trick your device into connecting to the Wi-Fi and Bluetooth devices they control. Once inside, hackers can spy on your activities, access your sensitive information, and even use your device to impersonate any app on your device, including the apps you use for online banking. Cybercriminals can also download data from your gadget if it is still within reach. Hackers can also see which networks your device has previously connected to; this is important because your phone considers these networks trusted and will automatically connect to them in the future.

Hackers can make phone calls and log into online accounts or apps without notifying the device owner. Cybercriminals may even install malware on your device to steal information from your gadgets. Hackers can install programs (Bluetooth or otherwise) and steal your information, including SIM card information used to access cellular communications.

Bluetooth hacking can happen when hackers use their own Bluetooth connection to gain access to your phone. Hackers hack into Bluetooth by installing specialized software and hardware that can detect vulnerable devices with active Bluetooth connections. Hackers use specialized software to automatically detect nearby Bluetooth devices. Fraudsters use specialized software to intercept your Bluetooth signal and hijack your device.

To log in, nearby hackers force your Bluetooth device to use weaker encryption when connected, making it more vulnerable to hackers. Using "professional" software and hardware, a hacker can intercept the Bluetooth handshake when the two devices connect and establish a connection, and quickly get into your device using different encryption methods. Most Bluetooth hacks can be done in a number of ways, either by infiltrating the network through a backdoor, or simply logging in by pairing it with one of your devices. To make matters worse, Bluetooth hackers can inject malware into your phone, transferring malicious code or viruses from one device to another.

Get it because Bluetooth is a relatively fragile technology for connecting many other devices. Yes, Bluetooth is one of the best features of our phone, but you should always use it with care. If you enable Bluetooth, it will continue to search for open devices within reachable range. Do not limit the security of any device through Bluetooth.

Its use prevents your Bluetooth connection from being discovered by other unknown devices. In most cases, users must allow the Bluetooth connection before exchanging data, a process called "pairing", which provides data security measures. Bluejacking devices (controlling sending messages to other nearby Bluetooth devices), Bluesnarfing (accessing or stealing data on Bluetooth devices), and Bluebugging (full control of Bluetooth devices) require different exploits and skill sets.

Windows users will find Bluetooth in Settings > Devices > Bluetooth (or you may have a shortcut in the taskbar). The current pairing can be found in your device's Bluetooth settings. Make sure that both the sending and receiving device's Bluetooth is turned on.

If you're sure your device is in pairing mode but doesn't appear in the list of devices on your computer, try turning Bluetooth off and on again. Tap on Bluetooth and you'll see a list of switched and paired devices (as well as currently connected devices). If you don't immediately see the device you want to connect to in the Bluetooth list, scroll down as it may be hidden below the menu. A common Bluetooth problem is that the device you're trying to pair doesn't appear in the list when searching for your phone.

Common problems with Bluetooth are usually caused by the Bluetooth device being turned off or not in pairing mode. If you have paired your Bluetooth device with multiple computers or other devices, this can cause conflicts and affect the connection. If your devices don't speak common Bluetooth languages, they won't connect. Apps can access data from your speakers and other connected devices even when your Bluetooth isn't broadcasting.

Even with Bluetooth discovery disabled, previously paired devices are still able to connect to the computer. After a device connects for the first time, pairing is usually remembered, and subsequent connections happen automatically, at least when both devices have Bluetooth turned on and are in close proximity to each other. By using this strategy, you have more control over the discoverability of your Bluetooth device, because you don't need to make the Bluetooth device discoverable to connect to a new headset after the initial pairing. During the pairing process, you can try to pair with another iPhone to determine if your Bluetooth problem is with your iPhone or the device you're trying to pair with.

Your Android phone will scan and discover nearby Bluetooth devices, and you can connect to them with anything. Many apps on your phone, such as Google and Facebook, also use Bluetooth to track the location of your device. Many apps, including popular ones from Facebook, Google, and others, use your device's Bluetooth capabilities to track your location.

Many automation apps, such as If This Then That and Tasker, can be set to turn off Bluetooth automatically when you leave a location or disconnect from a device. Turning Bluetooth wireless technology on and off also resets the setting and helps resolve any connection issues by having the computer search for nearby devices again. Disabling other nearby devices that are connected to your computer via Bluetooth may help resolve the connection issue. Unshielded USB devices can sometimes interfere with Bluetooth connections.

There are several things you can do to protect your Bluetooth enabled devices from these types of attacks. You can prevent anyone from connecting to your Bluetooth speaker using a security code, buying a better speaker, turning off the speaker when you're not using it, unpairing unwanted devices, updating software, and turning off visibility. If your speaker supports advanced settings, you can open Bluetooth, check the list of connected devices, and then "forget" them all.

To make your phone visible to other devices, open the basic Bluetooth settings. Swipe the Bluetooth button to the right so it turns green and tap Allow New Connections to connect to new devices. Press and hold the icon to go directly to the Bluetooth settings, where you will see a list of paired devices. In the [Add Device] window, select the Bluetooth headset you want to connect.

Press and hold (or right-click) the name of the Bluetooth adapter (which may contain the word "radio") and select Uninstall device > Uninstall. Uninstalling the network adapter If you don't see the Bluetooth icon, but Bluetooth appears in Device Manager, try uninstalling the Bluetooth adapter, and then turn on automatic reinstallation. Select to disable Bluetooth on your computer until you enable the Bluetooth adapter using Device Manager.

As with the device management method, users will need to open the Services app and enable Bluetooth if they want to use Bluetooth again. The undocumented solution is to require the user to disable and re-enable

Bluetooth on their device. The Services app should only be used if Bluetooth cannot be turned off using Action Center, Settings, or Device Manager.

To uninstall, open Settings > Connections > Bluetooth and turn on the toggle to see all previously paired devices. If the headset or speaker was previously paired with another phone, laptop, or tablet, turn off the other phone or Bluetooth. Your device may be paired but not connected—Bluetooth keyboards, mice, and pens only connect when needed.

Switching nearby Bluetooth devices to "stealth" mode will provide much better protection against unauthorized connections. For example, an important Bluetooth security feature is the ability for users to switch between "discoverable" and "stealth" modes. Another way for advanced users to disable Bluetooth is to use the Registry Editor. This is by far the easiest and most affordable way to turn off Bluetooth on Windows 10.

A user who wants their phone to connect to the car, but does not want their phone to use Bluetooth to discover it, will need to configure additional settings.

All Measures to Prevent Backdoors Connections of Windows

A backdoor is a technique used to bypass security protocols and gain unauthorized access to a system. Computer backdoors allow unauthorized users to easily gain advanced access to applications, networks, or devices. Backdoors allow attackers to use infected computers as if they were their own PCs and use them for various malicious purposes and even criminal activities. A backdoor not only allows a hacker to access your computer and network, but also allows him to come back and get into your system again and again.

Backdoors use security procedures and authentication to provide hackers with unauthorized remote access to your network. A backdoor is a malicious computer program used to provide an attacker with unauthorized remote access to an infected PC system by exploiting a security hole. A backdoor is a malicious port or application that provides access to a server or network. This enables criminals to perform any possible action on your computer.

Once installed, the backdoor can work independently and penetrate into the infected system, receiving commands from the attacker if necessary. Attackers can use it to spy on users, manage their files, install additional malware or dangerous scripts, take control of entire PC systems, and attack other hosts. Software and hardware developers or cybercriminals can install backdoors to gain unauthorized access to devices, install malware, steal user data, or disrupt networks.

Backdoors are a way for cybercriminals to access your devices in order to install malware. Backdoors can be installed manually by attackers who have the right to install software on your computers.

To avoid detection, backdoors can be programmed to change the protocols they use to connect to C&C servers. Once attackers find it, they can use backdoors to temporarily connect to the system and perform other malicious activities such as file transfers. The backdoors then infect all the profiles of those using the hacked computer.

Attackers can modify the backdoor to check for available insecure ports for communication. Often, attackers also use backdoors to inspect connections to bypass Intrusion Detection Systems (IDS). While many of these secret access methods are implemented by vendors and service providers, some backdoors create a vulnerability that can be exploited remotely, giving an attacker access to the root system.

Unfortunately, some known backdoors cannot be disabled and require additional security measures to reduce the threat. A number of security programs are available to remove backdoors, although some viruses may require scanning with several different antimalware tools. Monitor the network for suspicious connections In addition, administrators judiciously use vulnerability scanners or configuration management tools to identify known vulnerabilities and possibly detect and disable them. Add an extra layer of security to network monitoring as it is key to preventing backdoor attacks.

There are other ways to prevent backdoor attacks. Using an antivirus tool to detect Trojans, RATs, and other types of malware remains the most effective method. It is important to use reliable antivirus software to detect malware on your computer, mainly because hackers build backdoors into systems using RATs and Trojans. Modern antivirus software can help detect and prevent a variety of malware, including Trojans, ransomware hackers, spyware, and rootkits, which are often used by cybercriminals for backdoor attacks. Most antivirus programs come with firewalls that help prevent attacks such as backdoor viruses.

Security organizations may use backdoors to access protected systems. Attackers can use backdoors to gather information, take control of systems, or physically damage networks. Backdoor utilities are programmed through computers in the IT system that do not connect to the network very often. Even if your administrator changes passwords when an attack is detected, backdoor utilities can be programmed in such a way that a hacker can log into your system repeatedly.

These types of backdoors have "legitimate" uses, such as giving manufacturers a way to reset a user's password. Backdoors can also arise when people don't follow security best practices, such as using weak passwords to protect sensitive information or skipping two-factor authentication. Supply chain backdoors often attack networks and devices that carry sensitive information, making them particularly destructive.

Hackers use exploits to install malware (including backdoors) on user devices. Hackers can install backdoors on your system once malicious files have infected your device, or your device has been physically compromised (stolen or hacked) or targeted for exploits. In addition to these backdoor attacks, they also use various tactics to provide hackers with access as a camouflaged entry point.

From there, backdoors can be used to access privileged information, such as passwords, corrupt or delete data on hard drives, or transmit information over automated fabric networks. A backdoor can take the form of a hidden part of a program [3], a separate program (e.g., in the field of cybersecurity, a backdoor is a program where authorized and unauthorized users can bypass normal security measures and gain high access to computer systems, networks, or software applications) level of user access (also known as root access). By using a backdoor to gain root access to your system, cybercriminals can remotely control your computer by connecting it to a network of hacked computers, also known as a zombie The internet.

Backdoors are not dangerous in and of themselves, but once hackers can find them on your computer, they can use them to bypass your security mechanisms and gain unauthorized access to your system, which makes them quite dangerous. Backdoors are installed by viruses such as spyware or trojans without your knowledge.

An attacker could attempt to exploit the vulnerability by sending a specially crafted telnet packet to a Windows server and, if successful, execute arbitrary code on the server. The vulnerability could allow remote code execution if an attacker sends a specially crafted package to an affected Microsoft server. A buffer size checking vulnerability could allow an unauthenticated remote attacker to send specially crafted packets to a vulnerable device, resulting in a partial denial of service or remote code execution. An attacker who successfully exploited this vulnerability could gain root access to the target system.

The lack of buffer size checking allows a low-skilled attacker to gain full remote access to a vulnerable router. The error can be exploited by an unauthorized remote attacker who can convince an already logged in web interface user to follow a malicious link. `` Lack of buffer size checking could allow a remote attacker to bypass authentication.

A buffer overflow vulnerability exists in this service that could allow remote code execution. The vulnerability occurs when the Telnet service incorrectly validates user input. The security update addresses the vulnerability by correcting the way the service validates user input. If vulnerable devices accept Telnet connections, an attacker who sends invalid Telnet parameters when the connection is established can execute arbitrary code.

Many times when you try to use Telnet, your network may be blocking the connection. One of the most important things to remember is that the Telnet network protocol is disabled by default in Windows settings, so you need to enable it before you can do anything. Just like on Windows, you can access the Telnet network protocol through Terminal, Command Prompt in macOS 10.13 High Sierra. Users connect to the machine remotely using Telnet, sometimes called Telnet on the system.

The Telnet utility allows users to test connections to remote computers and enter commands using the keyboard. How Telnet Works Telnet is a client/server protocol that can be used to open a command prompt on a remote computer (usually a server). In this chapter, we will analyze how to use the Telnet network protocol to manage ports in Windows 10, Windows Server 2016, 2012 and 2008.

One of the biggest advantages of the Telnet network protocol is that with a simple command, you can check if a port is open. Users can open a command prompt on a remote machine, enter the word telnet and the name or IP address of the remote machine, and the telnet connection will ping the port to see if it is open or not. Users can also connect to any software that uses plain text protocols via Telnet, from web servers to ports.

FTP can also be used in conjunction with Telnet for users working on sending data files. While the basic operations of Shadowintegers Backdoor (SBD) remain more or less the same as other tools like Netcat, there are a couple of additional options that can be useful for file transfers.

If you're running in client mode, SBD allows you to specify the source port with the -p option (in server mode, -p specifies the listen port as usual). The original intention seems to be to use the Shadowintegers Backdoor (SBD) as the original chat client; however, it would also be useful to provide some kind of "tag" of data to register with the server. Shadowintegers Backdoor (SBD) is another Netcat variant with all the features of the original Netcat plus some new features. This particular version contained a backdoor that went undetected for months and was activated by sending the letters "AB" and a system command to the server on whatever port it was listening on.

This could allow an attacker to intercept network traffic, manage web SSH and backdoors, and create system accounts. Anyone from DDoS botnet operators to state-sponsored hacker and ransomware groups can use this backdoor account to gain access to vulnerable devices and traverse internal networks for further attacks, security experts warn. Attackers can use this account to log into a vulnerable device and run commands with full administrator rights. With a sufficient level of access, the creation of such accounts can be used to establish secondary access to credentials that does not require the deployment of permanent remote access tools on the system.

Backdoor services allow hackers to use elevated privileges, in most cases as a system account. A brute force attack can be used to quickly log in to multiple user accounts by exposing the list of users on that system, exploiting another vulnerability to obtain the passwd file, or listing those user IDs through Samba.

If such a program was installed on your computer by an attacker, that user will gain remote access to your computer. By gaining complete unauthorized control over your computer, an attacker can use your computer in almost any way. An attacker can change the way these programs run to get a command line or a backdoor without logging in.

To create a backdoor, hackers can use freely available commercial tools such as Remote Administrator [7] or TightVNC [8], which allow the use of a remote console in addition to full control of the computer. As with the One vulnerability (CVE-2020-15498), a remote attacker without a password could take full control of a vulnerable device. Remotely mapping a network drive (or using the net use command) from another machine is a way to see everything hidden from local users.

Hackers Attack You with Your IP Address!

Every device connected to the Internet has an IP address, which helps websites identify your computer. Someone can use your IP address to hack your device The Internet uses ports as well as your IP address to connect. Cybercriminals can find out your IP address by hacking into your home network or pasting a mistake into an HTML email.

Hackers can also use a combination of your IP address and data from other sources to piece together data about your identity. Others can piece together pieces of your identity by using your IP address and monitoring your online activity.

If hackers gain access to your computer through other means, such as malware, they can use your IP address to perform all sorts of shady activities on your behalf. While your IP address does not contain sensitive information such as a phone number or apartment location, hackers can still use your IP address against you. Your IP address gives a hacker the freedom to use your location for any kind of manipulative activity and can also attack your device with malware.

Based on your IP address, the IP address prevents hackers from controlling your computer or impersonating you on the Internet. Your IP address cannot be used to reveal your specific identity or location, or to hack or remotely control your computer.

You can use the IP address to find out where a computer came from, such as its country of origin. Since ISPs often assign hostnames to their devices using geographic names, we can get more information about the location of a potential hacker's IP address. This IP address can be used to determine the remote user's approximate geographic location, the login name, possibly from their computer, and the hostname authentication key.

If any of the IP addresses do not match, it means that they have been used by an attacker. It will take a little more detective work to match your devices' IP addresses to those listed.

Of course, you can always find out the IP address of the device you're using, for example, the IP address of your printer. If someone borrows or uses your computer, they can find your IP address in seconds because there are many free websites that allow you to do this.

There are many Linux commands and tools that can determine the IP address of any computer trying to establish a connection. You can find the IP address of anyone trying to hack your site in hosting logs, Google Analytics or other analytics tools. You can try a tool like NetStat to determine the IP address of anyone trying to connect to your computer.

When using a VPN, if someone tries to determine your IP address, they will only see the IP address of the server from which you connect to the Internet, which may be in another country, in your country, or on the other side of the world. Therefore, it is recommended that you keep your IP address secret from people you don't know. In most cases, you cannot be harmed by someone who knows your IP address. However, if it falls into the wrong hands, your computer can be scanned and your computer checked for vulnerabilities that allow someone to access your data.

What to do if someone has your IP address You cannot prevent someone from using your IP address if they have one; just like you can't stop someone from using your social security number if you lose your social security card. There are thousands of ports for every IP address, and a hacker who has your IP address can try all of these ports to force a connection, such as hijacking your phone and stealing your information. The first way predators get into your network is by looking for weak IP addresses. In a DoS attack, hackers use fake IP addresses to flood computer servers with data packets, shutting them down.

Hackers can also perform distributed denial-of-service (DDoS) attacks by flooding the network with data through IP addresses and overloading the network to prevent traffic from flowing normally. The most common method of this type of attack is to flood your address with server requests, overloading and crippling your system with traffic. Knowing your IP address, an attacker can perform a denial of service (DoS) attack that floods your network with data.

Overcoming this type of attack can be even more difficult due to the fact that the attacker appears simultaneously from many different IP addresses around the world, making it even more difficult for network administrators to determine the source of the attack. A hacker could potentially be using a local IP address but actually being on the other side of the world. Instead, IP addresses can reveal your city, zip code, or area code where you are currently connecting to the Internet—which is why IP addresses change every time you connect from a new location or use a new router.

This hint is useful during port forwarding if you want to send some data directly from the router to the computer's IP address. Using it will help protect your device from IP address hacking. An IP address can be thought of as the numerical address of a device connected to the Internet because it shows your geographic location to help the Internet serve content relevant to you.

The devices we connect to the Internet also have unique identifiers - Internet Protocol addresses, commonly referred to as IP addresses. Essentially, an IP address is how computers on the Internet identify each other. In fact, every website you visit already knows your IP address - that's how they know how to start your computer and not someone else's.

Change Your Computer Name and IP Address Often To Dodge Attacks

The easiest way to reset your public and private IP address is to turn your router off and on again, and if a modem is present, the modem. To change the Linksys IP address, you need to hard reset your router. After reconnecting your router, update the IP management site to make sure your IP address has changed.

Verify that the change has taken effect by using your IP address to access the router's settings page. Typically, when you perform a hard reset on a router, all settings will be reset to default and the router will also be assigned a new public IP address different from the one it was using before the reset. Generally, a quick router restart (soft reset) does not change the IP address, but factory resets or ISP service resets change the public IP address assigned to the router. Let's analyze the issue in more detail, distinguishing between the different types of reboots/resets that a router can perform and how the public IP address can sometimes be changed on different occasions.

A common problem with home routers is that they sometimes give devices the wrong IP address, so manually changing the IP address can fix these issues. A failed router provides incorrect addresses, such as an address used by another computer on the network. In most cases, the reason for the sudden change of IP address is usually a failure between the router and the Internet. For example, in rare cases it may be necessary to change the local IP address to avoid conflict with another device on the network.

There may be reasons to change your public or local IP address from time to time. You can change your local IP address in the network settings management menu on a PC, Mac, or phone. If necessary, you can change the IP address of your phone or computer at any time by going to your device's settings. Please note that changing your IP address will temporarily stop any Internet-connected services or programs you are using on your device.

Change your local IP address if you're trying to troubleshoot internet problems or hide other devices that are connected to the same internet connection as you. If you want to get a new IP address to protect yourself from people who might be following you online, your best bet is to try resetting your internet connection. Changing the IP address of a router on the local network is useful for certain situations, such as cascading to another router or preventing IP conflicts with a modem.

This article also explains how to change the router's public IP address, which appears as the public IP address of every device on the network, unless you're using a VPN. Any computer connected to your network will have different private addresses assigned by your router, but only one public address. Public IP address. It is sometimes called the gateway IP address. This address is assigned by your ISP and is on your router or firewall. The second part is the private address assigned to your computer, which is in a series of private IPs that don't have internet access, your router assigns you a private address and uses it when you communicate with the website/system/server convert. on the Internet.

Typically, the internal IP address of computers, phones, and other devices connected to the Internet is provided by a DHCP server, which is usually a modem/router. The external IP address of the modem/router that provides Internet connectivity in your home or office is provided by your Internet Service Provider (ISP). Internal IP Addresses: The router will assign an individual address to each device connected to the local area network (LAN).

If you make sure your modem or router's IP address is correct, you can set a static IP address on your computer or smartphone to tell it where to connect. If you exit the automatic IP address setting, the router will automatically assign an IP address to the computer. Change the IP address or select Obtain an IP address automatically to have the router check the IP address. After that, copy the router's IP address field to an IPv4 address and change the last set number to any number between 1 and 255.

Another way to change the IP address is to turn off the modem/router and turn it back on after 5 minutes. After you change the IP address of your Linksys router, you may need to update your computer's IP address to reconnect. To resolve an internet connection issue that wasn't resolved by restarting your router, try releasing and renewing your IP address.

The quickest and easiest way to get a new IP address is to find out what your IP address is through the IP address management site, then go to your router and turn it off for at least five minutes. If you just want to change your IP address without increasing your privacy further, you can manually enter your preferred IP address or just have your device get a new one automatically.

YOUR SYSTEM'S SWEETSPOTS: CEO'S ADVICE ON BASIC CYBER SECURITY

It's possible and easy to set static private IP addresses on routers for individual devices in the home - see our article which covers game consoles, but this applies to all devices - but here we intend to fix public/external IP addresses your router to the location, for this you need to contact your provider. This article describes how to manually change the IP address from the DHCP assigned to the router to a static IP address on Windows, Mac, iOS, and Android. This is the default IP address from which you can log into the wireless modem or router to change settings, change the WiFi name or password. Manufacturers typically use the base IP address (many use 192.168.0.1) used to log into the router's login page.

Internet Protocol (IP) addresses identify a device on a local area network or a network that is not connected to the Internet. The number of different public IPv4 addresses is limited and is usually assigned to the device by the Internet Service Provider (ISP). Millions of private networks around the world use reserved IP addresses in specific IPv4 address ranges.

An IP address is considered private if the IP number falls within one of the IP address ranges reserved for private networks, such as a local area network (LAN). Home and corporate networks use private or internal addresses from a special range of IP addresses. Some IP addresses are reserved for public use, while others are reserved for private use.

When discussing IP addresses, you've probably heard the terms "public" and "private". The terms "public" and "private" refer to the location of the network, i.e. the private IP address is used inside the network and the public IP address is used outside the network. Private means that the IP address can only be accessed by other devices on the same network.

The router will be assigned a public IP address, but then each device on the home network will be assigned a private address using DHCP. The desktop computer will communicate with each other using its private IP address, and the central router will use its public IP address to facilitate communication over the Internet. When you open a website from your computer, a request is sent from your computer to your home router as a private IP address, after which the router requests the website from your ISP using the public IP address assigned to your network. Devices outside the local network cannot communicate directly through their private IP address, but use the router's public IP address to communicate.

Instead of assigning every device on your home network a public IP address, the only public IP address you will use is assigned to the central router. The router you use to connect to the Internet assigns a private IP address to every device on the same network (2 computers and 3 mobile phones in our example). Network routers are also assigned private IP addresses and use them to route web traffic internally.

Each device on your home network has a unique private IP address that helps the router deliver instructions or redirect traffic from the Internet to the right device. A private IP address allows a router to properly route traffic on its network, and private IP addresses also allow devices within a network to communicate with each other. Every device connected to the Internet has an Internet Protocol address, or IP address, and both private and public IP addresses are equally important.

Understanding how both types of IP addresses work will help you appreciate the modern Internet. NAT allows thousands of computers on an internal network to access the Internet using a single external IP address. In home and small office networks, a NAT router connects the internal network to the Internet using a single public or public routable IP address assigned by the ISP from a dedicated block of addresses.

The ISP provides the customer with a private WAN IP address and then uses NAT to distinguish which host the packet should be directed to. From the example above, you can see that with dynamic IP addresses, the ISP provides the router with private WAN IP addresses, which are then "translated" to public IP addresses when the router connects to a remote host on the Internet. The example above shows a scenario where Internet Service Providers (ISPs) provide different routers with unique and permanent IP addresses (they never change for each device). Internet Service Provider (ISP) IP addresses are unique and permanent (remember, it's the ISP that assigns your router a public IP address, it doesn't matter that the router assigns private IP addresses to all the devices on your home or corporate network .

And so on (the IP address is usually reserved for the router itself). You can assign a specific IP address to the device in the router's control panel so that the device always gets the same local IP address when connected. You usually don't need to know the local IP address unless you're trying to set up a game or web server. The local IP address may change based on other devices connected to the same network and the order in which they were connected. When you're at home, you have a different IP address, and when you're at the library or anywhere else, you have a different IP address.

Internal IP addresses are used for the local internal network, and external IP addresses are used to communicate with machines on the Internet. A local or internal IP address is used on a private network to locate computers and devices connected to it. Your Internet Service Provider (ISP) assigns you an external IP address when you connect to the Internet.

All devices with unique internal IP addresses are connected to the Internet through a local network, and no one outside the network can access them. Private IP addresses can be assigned to your computer, phone, tablet, or any other device on your private network without exposing your computer to the Internet world. In a typical network, routers use your public IP address to identify you to the rest of the Internet, ensuring that email, websites, streaming content, and other data are delivered correctly. An IP address is a unique identifier on the network and is used to send and receive information on the network.

On Windows 10, you can also change IP address settings using the Wireless and wired adapter's Settings app. For an extra layer of security, you can change your router's IP address. The IP address assigned by the router is dynamic in nature and changes every time the device reboots.

The reason is that, by default, connected devices use a dynamic IP address assigned by a Dynamic Host Configuration Protocol (DHCP) server (usually a router), which may change at any time once the machine is rebooted or configured. Allocation expires. A common problem with home routers is that they sometimes give devices the wrong IP address, so manually changing the IP address can fix these problems. Please note that changing your IP address will temporarily suspend any internet services or programs you use on your device.

If you just want to change your IP address without further increasing your privacy, you can manually enter your preferred IP address or let your device automatically obtain a new one. If you want to switch to using an IP address automatically assigned by a DHCP server instead of a static IP address, use the command netsh interface ipv4 set address name = "YOUR INTERFACE NAME" source = dhcp.

Select the Obtain an IP address automatically option and Windows 10 will look for a DHCP server the next time the system boots. Type ipconfig /renew at the prompt window, wait a few seconds, the DHCP server will assign a new IP address for your computer.

Select Use the following IP address, enter the required details (8 and 9 in the image above), and click OK. that's all. On the IPv4 Properties screen, select Use the following IP address settings > Enter default gateway (DHCP server address), subnet mask address, new IP address, and then click OK. This command will use the WiFi interface, set the IP address to 192.168.0.173, the subnet mask to 255.255.255.0, and the default gateway to 192.168.0.0.

In the Wi-Fi Settings window, scroll down to the Properties section and find the IPv4 address in the Properties section. To view the IP address of a wired connection, select Ethernet from the left menu bar and select your network connection. Your IP address will appear next to "IPv4 Address". Another window will open showing the items used by your internet connection.

Your new IP address will appear here, but go to the bottom of the screen and click Advanced, then click IP Settings. Check your IP address through a website such as WhatIsMyIP.network to make sure the changes have been made. Changing the IP address using the control panel interface is not difficult, but it requires clicking on many different windows and dialogs.

You can make changes using the Windows 10 Settings app, Control Panel, PowerShell or Command Prompt and network DHCP settings. Windows PowerShell will allow you to release or renew your Windows IP address before making any changes to the router's DHCP settings. Windows 10 also includes the PowerShell command line platform, which allows you to use the "NetTCPIP" module to manage your network settings, including the ability to change your computer's IP address settings.

In Windows 10, setting a static IP address on a computer is a configuration that may need to be adjusted in many scenarios. Although using commands can be difficult for some users, this is one of the fastest ways to set a static IP address in Windows 10. Whichever method is used, it is recommended that you assign an IP address within and outside the network range. DHCP server to ensure adequate connectivity and avoid address conflicts.

YOUR SYSTEM'S SWEETSPOTS: CEO'S ADVICE ON BASIC CYBER SECURITY

In any event, such written notice must include your name, address, and an express statement that you do not wish to resolve disputes with Belkin International through arbitration. This agreement takes effect when you click the "I agree" button or when you otherwise use, copy or install the software, which means you agree and accept this agreement. As part of the license, you may (A) use the software as described in the software user documentation; (B) if the software is offered for download on a personal computer or mobile device, make all aspects of the software reasonably necessary for your personal use copies (this does not include firmware); (C) irrevocably assigns all rights in your use of our Belkin products (including but not limited to software) to another person, provided that person also agrees to be bound by this Agreement, and discontinue use of the Product after such transfer. and software.

You can apply random hardware MAC addresses to all Wi-Fi networks or to a single Wi-Fi network to connect to. When this feature is enabled for a specific network, a random hardware address will be used the next time you connect to that network. As mentioned above, Windows 11 can use random hardware MAC addresses when connecting to Wi-Fi networks to prevent Wi-Fi networks from tracking your computer's MAC address and your location.

When the computer is locked out of the network based on this MAC address, if you manage to unlock it, it may render the network connection unusable. If you continue to use the same random MAC address for each connection, the hotel's Wi-Fi will recognize you and you won't have to fill out the form, or in the worst case, pay for the connection again. For reconnects, by default, the system will continue to use the same MAC address the system used on the first connection, randomization if randomization is enabled for the first connection, or persistent if randomization is disabled.

If the new network is a new network and randomization is enabled, a random MAC address will be chosen for the network and used for new connections. If set to On, registering to a new network will generate a random address that will always be used for that network. At this point, if this is the first time connecting to a new network, or if you have already connected to the same network in the past, the system will behave differently.

As soon as you connect to a network, MAC address randomization stops to maintain a stable connection. Starting with Android 10, MAC address randomization is enabled by default when connecting to a new network. Most Android and Windows devices also have automatic MAC address randomization, but you may need to check if it is enabled.

When it comes to MAC address security, MAC address randomization is probably the best method to use. Instead of setting a fake address, MAC randomization allows you to cycle through random fake addresses when not connected to Wi-Fi. When setting random hardware addresses in Windows 10, you can use a new address at the beginning of each day or at the beginning of each new connection.

After completing these steps, the computer uses a random hardware address when scanning for networks and connects to any Wi-Fi hotspot. After completing these steps, the device will use a random MAC address when connecting to the wireless network. This feature is included in Windows 10, and by following these simple steps, Windows 10 will allow your computer to tell your router a random MAC address every time your computer requests a connection.

The membership request will include your machine's unique physical hardware (MAC) address. A MAC address (short for "Media Access Control") is a series of numbers and letters that identify a network device. The difference between a MAC address and an IP address is that a MAC address never changes and is only used on a local network, whereas an IP address identifies network devices globally and can change based on your location. If you want to connect to the Internet or send and receive information, our devices need to know the address of each device and the network they are connected to.

The router will then assign you an IP address and allow you to connect to the Internet. Go to the start tile > Settings > Network & Internet > Wi-Fi connections. In Settings -> Network and Internet -> Status I see my private network.

In the network state, I have a network connection set up with the name of my WiFi network and connected to 2 computers in my house. Even if you don't connect to any of the hundreds of networks, your device keeps sending them to discover surrounding networks and list them for you. Usually, when your device is not connected, it wakes up every minute or two and tries to find out if there is an available Wi-Fi network nearby.

"Stable" mode still makes you easily recognizable when you reconnect to a previous network, but your hardware MAC address is hidden and it might be harder to find you on other networks (YMMV). Leaving the Random Address option set to "Off" means that all connections will use the normal MAC address of the NICs. This is similar to macchanger:random, except that NetworkManager uses the constant MAC address of the devices and macchanger keeps the current OUI address.

Note that the "connection.stable-id" property is also used to generate IPv6 addresses with stable privacy ("ipv6.addr-gen-mode", RFC 7217). Stable addresses are generated by hashing the private key from /var/lib/ NetworkManager/secret_key, the device's ifname and stable ID. Publishing stable and temporary addresses in DNS, or anywhere else where they are related to each other by a common identifier, can match the actions of a host when either address is used.

Temporary addresses use randomly generated IIDs and change daily by default. Tools such as macchanger and macchiato support flexible mechanisms for generating random addresses, most of these options are now also supported by NetworkManager.

The privacy and security properties of the address generation mechanism Section 3 depend on how each host address is generated and used. Hosts that use static IPv4 addressing or are permanently assigned the same address via DHCPv4 can be controlled as described above.

Other mechanisms (eg [RFC 7596], [RFC 7597], [RFC 7599]) fall somewhere in between, using an IPv4 address and a port set identifier (which is not randomized for many NATs).

The 24-bit Organizationally Unique Identifier (OUI) of the MAC address, together with the fixed values (0xff, 0xfe) used to form the modified EUI-64 interface ID, greatly helps reduce the search space, making it easier for attackers to find scans. A single address using the well-known OUI.

How to Hide Your Computer From Internet

There are several ways to hide your computers from the internet.

The best security measure you can take when connecting to a public Wi-Fi network is to change your IP address. Remember, hiding your Wi-Fi network is not an effective security measure. To increase the security of your network, you might consider hiding the name of your Wi-Fi network so that people nearby cannot connect to your Wi-Fi network. Because if you don't use the default public IP address, it will be very difficult for an attacker to track you down.

Your IP address is assigned to you by your ISP, so if you connect to the Internet through a different network, you will be assigned a new one. IP address Your IP address identifies your device on the Internet or on a local network. An address or Internet Protocol (IP) is a unique string of numbers and decimals used to identify each device that connects to the Internet. Since your computer and other devices require an IP address to access information on the Internet, it is impossible to completely avoid using an IP address.

When using a VPN, the only entity that can associate your online activity with your IP address is your VPN provider. When you connect your computer (or other device, such as a smartphone or tablet) to the VPN, the computer behaves as if it were on the same local network as the VPN. When you connect to a virtual private network (VPN), you create a virtual tunnel that not only encrypts your data, but also uses the VPN server's IP address.

A virtual private network (VPN) can hide a user's internal protocol (IP) address and block their location and browsing history, allowing them to share and receive information over public internet networks more privately. The two main ways to hide your IP address are by using a proxy server or by using a virtual private network (VPN). You can virtually hide yourself using a virtual private network before connecting to a website or web page.

If you connect to the Internet through unsecured networks, such as those in coffee shops and airports, you can set your connection to "Public" to hide your device in that location and turn off file and printer sharing. You can connect to public or private Wi-Fi networks, or use your smartphone's mobile data connection. If you don't have easy access to a public Wi-Fi connection, or don't want to expose yourself to all the risks that come with public Wi-Fi, you can also temporarily change your IP address using data on your mobile device instead of Wi-Fi. Philip. .Any devices already connected to your wireless network should remain connected, but you will need to manually enter the Wi-Fi network name when connecting new devices in the future.

A list of available network connections and their types will be displayed, click on the desired network connection type and change it to "Public Network" in the new window. In the first case, click on the network connection icon in the notification area, and in the window that opens, click on the "Network and Internet Settings" item. A new window will open, select "Ethernet" in the left panel menu, then click the network connection whose availability you want to change in the right block.

To do this, we have to go to Start, write Control Panel, go to Networks and Internet, then to Network Centers and Shares and once here we go to Change settings for advanced usage.

If you share resources with others, these settings will make your job more difficult. To make your computer visible to other devices connected to the same local network, follow steps 1 to 3, and then check the box. You can disable network discovery, which will prevent other computers on your local network from connecting to your computer except through an IP address. When you connect to a trusted network, such as at home or at work, you can set the connection to "private" to make your computer discoverable and give network users access to resources you can share. Because your computer behaves as if it were online, this allows you to securely access local network resources even if you are on the other side of the world.

When you surf the web while connected to a VPN, your computer connects to websites through an encrypted VPN connection. A VPN prevents your ISP from seeing what you do online by hiding your IP address from the apps and websites you use, so no one can see the whole picture. A VPN is an intermediate server that encrypts your Internet connection and hides your IP address. While you can never hide your real IP address from your ISP, you can use a VPN to hide the content and destination of your internet activity.

IP addresses can also be used to track users' approximate location and online activity, so hiding is a must if you want to keep online privacy. After all, the only way to hide your IP address and continue to use the Internet is to disguise it as a different one. Hiding is a fairly easy way to change your IP address, but it won't solve any geo-blocking or security issues like a VPN would. This will keep non-tech-savvy people from trying to connect to your Wi-Fi network, but nothing more.

Interestingly, if we connect to a public network, which would then be a guest or public profile, we don't have the public network set up so that the computer is visible. As we know, it is possible that other computers connected to our network can see that we are connected. In particular, this means that anyone connected to the same network can access your personal data. We can find a private profile, which will be, for example, when connected to a home network, as well as a public or guest profile, which will be if we connect to a cafe or any place where there can be several users.

Stop USB Autorun/ Autoplay Function

As stated earlier, the Windows autorun feature is primarily intended to automatically launch applications distributed on CD/DVD, but can also be used for the same purpose on USB-based removable media. As a feature first introduced in Windows 95, AutoRun for USB drives worked... well, pretty well, especially considering how long malware has been using it as a distribution method. This is a real-time protection for USB drives, which should be used if you want to protect yourself from malware that uses the autorun feature to spread and infect other computers.

Autorun.in is a virus that usually spreads through infected external devices such as USB sticks. Once an infected USB drive enters your system, the virus can destroy your computer, launch self-executing files, destroy important documents, and replicate itself in a way that makes it difficult to remove.

The malicious autorun.inf file is used to trick users into running malware on infected USB drives. If you insert a USB flash drive, CD or DVD containing the Autorun.INF file into the root folder, Windows will automatically run all executables defined in Autorun.INF. Autorun Protection is similar to Microsoft Update KB971029 in that any USB sticks, CDs or DVDs, and other devices that will use the autorun.inf file will not be able to autostart.

Autorun works like this: when using removable media such as USB key, CD, etc., Microsoft automatically looks for a file named "autorun.inf" and if it is present, Windows performs the actions specified in the file. The file named AUTORUN is used to automatically launch AUTORUN each time an infected drive is accessed. A file called autorun.inf tells the Windows shell what to do and how to load data on the device or drive it is associated with. Usually, when a virus infects a Windows system causing problems opening a drive, it automatically creates a file called autorun.

The virus can also be embedded in what looks like a regular file on a USB device, so that even if autorun is disabled, your computer will be infected when you open the file. The USB drive will then spread the virus to other computers if the operating system on those computers has an autorun type feature enabled.

Autorun or AutoPlay on removable USB drives is no longer allowed, even if you plug the USB drive into another computer. Disabling autorun and the autorun feature prevents malicious code-infected external media from automatically launching on your computer. Microsoft Windows Enable autorun on Microsoft Windows systems.

Disabling AutoPlay on Microsoft Windows systems Microsoft Windows can help prevent the spread of malicious code. Since malware can take advantage of the Windows autorun feature, spreading a virus from an external device to the computer, many users choose to disable it. Disabling autorun on Microsoft Windows systems, detailed on the CERT/CC Vulnerability Analysis blog, is an effective way to prevent the spread of malicious code. Although the documentation for the NoDriveTypeAutoRun registry value states that Microsoft will not use autorun functionality on USB mass storage devices, this does not necessarily mean that users can safely plug any USB device into their system.

The NoDriveTypeAutoRun registry entry and the value of the NoDriveTypeAutoRun registry entry determine which drive or drives autorun will be disabled. Even with the autorun registry value set, Microsoft Windows can execute arbitrary code when the user clicks the device icon in Windows Explorer. Windows Vista and Windows Server 2008 will still prompt the user to run the AutoPlay command if the feature is configured to disable AutoPlay for the Network Drive feature, or if this policy is not configured.

Without security updates for Windows, it is not possible to disable autoplay for a network drive. In versions of Windows prior to Windows Vista, when you insert media that contains an AutoPlay command, the system automatically starts the program without user intervention. An administrator can disable the autorun commands entirely, or revert to pre-Windows Vista behavior so that the autorun command runs automatically.

For USB drives that contain an autorun.inf file, the program will not start automatically, but the option will appear in the autorun window. When you insert the software CD into your computer, Windows automatically reads the CD, and if the autorun.inf file is found in the root directory of the CD, Windows automatically starts the program specified in the autorun.inf file. The autorun.inf file used on the USB media drive requires a slightly different configuration to automatically run the application. However, even without it, a malicious autorun.inf file can trick people into running malware from a USB drive.

YOUR SYSTEM'S SWEETSPOTS: CEO'S ADVICE ON BASIC CYBER SECURITY

If you plug a malicious USB drive into your computer, you're still a click away from launching the malware via the autorun dialog, at least with the default settings. If you wish, you can disable AutoPlay completely or only for certain types of drives so that you don't see the AutoPlay pop-up when you insert removable media into your computer. The behavior of autorun can be unexpected, as it is generally assumed that clicking on the drive icon will display the contents of the drive, not run code.

If AutoRun is not present, the user will have to open a file browser window, navigate to the disk, and run setup.exe from there. In Windows 7, the autoplay feature for USB drives is disabled (the new OS will still autoplay all inserted CDs and DVDs).

In Windows 10, AutoPlay is a feature that lets you choose a default action when you connect a USB drive, memory card, and other types of media or devices to your computer. So you can "disable" Windows AutoPlay for certain types of devices without taking any action, but leaving it enabled for other devices. You can also hold down the Shift key while connecting your device to open the autoplay notification, regardless of the default setting. If you don't like the autoplay menu that pops up all the time, you can turn it off or set each device to do what you want it to do whenever it's plugged in.

You can disable AutoPlay in a few steps, but the process depends on your version of Windows. In Windows Vista, AutoPlay cannot bypass AutoPlay in this way; AutoStart can only be added to the options presented to the user. Because malware can take advantage of the Windows Autorun feature to spread viruses from external devices to the computer, many users choose to disable it.

Windows cannot run autorun, and you can disable all autoruns or leave autorun enabled only for CD/DVD drives. Autorun is a Windows feature that can automatically start a program located on an external source (such as a CD, USB drive, or network drive).

Autorun.in can both automatically launch programs and determine what actions they will perform automatically. Instead of letting autorun run the program automatically, autorun opens a window where you can choose whether and how you want to run the program on an external device.

Autoplay, which allows you to play or launch programs as soon as multimedia devices are connected to your computer (this feature is enabled by default in Windows 10). Windows 10 AutoPlay makes it easy to set up

AutoPlay actions for external devices connected to your PC. If you find this feature useless, or want to change the default settings to take a different action when you plug in a USB drive or other media or device, you can quickly control this feature using the Settings app or Control Panel.

We have helped users with several manual ways to manage the settings of AutoPlay and AutoPlay features on Windows 10 systems to specify what to do when an external drive is connected to the Windows 10 system. There are several ways to disable AutoPlay and AutoPlay features. and you can use any of them to run Turn. All of the above manual settings and procedures to disable AutoPlay and AutoPlay in Windows 10 AutoPlay and AutoPlay in Windows 10 can be easily performed by users if you follow each step carefully.

In this Windows 10 guide, we'll show you how to enable, disable, and configure default AutoPlay settings for removable media and AutoPlay defaults for removable media. For example, you can set the Windows autorun behavior for removable drives and camera memory, while Windows 7 does not support this media type. Because some types of devices do not have a drive letter, AutoPlay properties cannot be accessed or changed through My Computer.

Since Windows 98 cannot capture content on non-volume devices, AutoPlay scans these devices based on their characteristics, not content. Windows 98 looks up device properties or media content so that AutoPlay can provide the user with a meaningful set of options. Autorun is actually an extra layer of "security" between malware and your computer, as it requires your intervention before anything can actually be done. AutoPlay (also known as AutoRun) is a feature that automatically launches a program or opens a file on a removable drive or CD/DVD after plugging/inserting it.

AutoPlay is a Windows feature first introduced in Windows 98 that checks the content of any attached storage device or inserted media (for example, AutoPlay is a subkey of the AutoPlay feature enabled by default in Windows 10 that allows you to run media files). When connecting to an external device. Autoplay is a feature introduced in Windows 98 Windows 98 checks for newly discovered removable media and devices and launches the appropriate application to play or view the content (such as pictures) based on the content (such as pictures, music or video files) . , Simplified modern application with user interface allows you to disable autoplay completely, use autoplay for all media and devices only by using the slider, or select an action for removable drives and memory cards.

To completely disable AutoPlay/AutoPlay in Windows Vista, 7, Windows 8, and Windows 8.1, uncheck Use AutoPlay for all media and devices. In Windows 7 and 8, AutoPlay is disabled by default for all devices except CD/DVD media, although you can use a slightly different AutoPlay feature on USB devices. Windows 10 systems with AutoPlay or AutoRun enabled are vulnerable to malware attacks that cause data loss and corruption if a USB drive with malware is inserted into the computer (even if it is locked).

Autorun, on the other hand, is an operating system action that automatically launches the application according to the command specified in the autorun.inf file when we double-click the removable drive icon. This 7KB USB antivirus tool is loaded into the system tray and you can enable or disable autorun with one click. Autorun Vaccine is portable and can be placed in a tray while running. Tray menu options are available for auto inoculation as well as disabling auto play options.

Device Security: Core Isolation

A subset of one of these features is a feature called "Memory Integrity" that protects memory from malicious code injection via malware or malicious attacks. You can see if your PC has kernel isolation features enabled, and enable or disable Memory Integrity Protection from the Windows Defender Security Center app. Starting with Windows 10 Build 17093, you can configure Memory Health Core Isolation using the Windows Defender Security Center.

If you have core isolation enabled on your PC hardware, you will see the message "Virtualization-based security protects critical parts of the device" here. The Core Isolation feature provides many virtualization-based security options to protect critical parts of your computer. When certain kernel isolation features are enabled, Windows 10 uses hardware virtualization features to create a protected area of system memory that is isolated from the normal operating system.

Virtualization Based Security (VBS) uses the Windows hypervisor to virtually isolate a segment of main memory from the rest of the operating system, the operating system. Even if malware is running on your PC and knows an exploit that should allow it to disrupt important operating system processes, virtualization-based security is an additional layer of protection that isolates them from attacks. In short, Microsoft needs virtualization-based security to minimize the risk of malware in kernel mode, in addition to handling malicious code in user mode.

They use virtualization-based security to protect core operating system processes from unauthorized access, but memory protection is disabled by default for people performing updates. Core isolation is a security feature in the Windows 10 operating system that uses virtualization technology to protect Windows 10. Device security: Provides hardware-level security features such as core isolation and processor security to protect your computer from certain attacks.

The device security module provides hardware-level security, such as Secure Boot, which prevents malware from loading when the computer starts. Windows Security offers the following built-in security options to help protect your device from malware attacks. To access the features described below, in the search box on the taskbar, type "Windows Security", select "Windows Security" in the results, then select "Device Security". To open Windows Security, you can find it in the Start Menu or Settings, go to Update & Security and click on Windows Security on the left and then click on Open Windows Security.

Go to Start > Settings > Update & Security > Windows Security > Device Security, then under Core Isolation, click Core Isolation Details to open the Core Isolation page. You can click Firewall and Network Protection to access firewall settings. On the home page, you can view the security status of various security features that are available by default in Windows 10. On the home page, you can view the security status of various parts of Windows 11 as a whole.

Here, you'll learn how to optimize Windows Defender focus settings and protect your system from unwanted programs. With the steps and instructions above, you will be able to take full advantage of Windows Defender and protect your PC from any unwanted programs. No download required: Microsoft Windows Defender comes standard with Windows 10, protecting your data and devices in real-time with a comprehensive suite of advanced security measures. When Windows Defender is activated, Windows Defender provides firewall, folder protection, browser control, device driver protection, and virus protection.

Windows Firewall also protects you from hackers who might gain unauthorized access to your system. It offers protection against exploits and zero-day vulnerabilities, ensuring that all software running in kernel mode, including drivers, safely allocates memory and functions properly. Memory Integrity uses hardware virtualization and Hyper-V to protect Windows 10 kernel mode processes from injecting and executing malicious or unverified code. Memory Integrity (also known as Hypervisor Protected Code Integrity or HVCI) uses the Microsoft Hyper-V hypervisor to virtualize the hardware that runs certain Windows kernel model processes, protecting them from malicious code injection.

Memory integrity is a core isolation security feature that prevents attacks from injecting malicious code into highly secure processes. Memory Integrity is a core isolation feature that regularly checks the integrity of the code that runs critical core Windows processes in an attempt to prevent them from interfering with attacks. `` Kernel isolation is a Microsoft Windows security feature that protects critical Windows kernel processes from malicious software by isolating them in memory. Kernel isolation and memory integrity are just a few of the many new security features that Microsoft has added as part of Windows Defender Exploit Guard.

Windows Defender protects device drivers and protects them from malware threats with Core Isolation and Safe Boot. Windows Defender can protect your device, but it's wise to keep your drivers up to date and prevent security breaches. Security updates and outdated drivers can expose your device to malware attacks and vulnerabilities. Driver Security fixes vulnerabilities that could expose your computer to unwanted software.

Improving Hardware Security If your device's security capabilities do not meet your expectations, you may need to enable some hardware features (such as secure boot if supported) or change settings in your system's BIOS. The firmware must support virtualization, which allows a Windows 11/10 PC to run applications in a container so that they do not access other parts of the system.

Microsoft Windows has a feature that allows drivers to use HVCI, but such drivers must be written in a way that ensures a clear separation between data and code, and cannot load data files as executables or use dynamic code in the kernel . The HVCI service in Windows 10 determines whether code running in kernel mode is safe and trustworthy. When Memory Integrity is enabled, the Code Integrity Service in Windows 10 runs inside a hypervisor-protected container created by Core Isolation.

How to Encrypt Files in Your Computer

If you want to encrypt a file or folder in Windows 10 Pro, search and right-click first. In Windows Explorer, right-click the file or folder you want to encrypt. Typically, however, after installation, you will be able to find the files and folders you want to protect in Windows File Manager, then right-click on those files to select the files and folders you want to use with .

If you have created an archive to protect files or folders on your system, you should proceed to the section titled "Deleting any unencrypted copies of a file" once you have finished encrypting the files, and follow the instructions there to make sure that you are not lying there. unencrypted copies of things where some curious person can find them. To be on the safe side, you'll want to delete any temporary files after you've finished encryption. Files encrypted with the methods below can still be deleted, so you may want to have a backup somewhere else. Again, keep an unencrypted backup of the file on a physical drive in a safe place where it can't be found.

If you encrypt one file, your computer will store an unencrypted version of that file in temporary memory so that a skilled spy can access it. One disadvantage of Microsoft Office Suite encryption is that unencrypted versions of recently opened files can be stored in your computer's temporary memory. If you're using 7-zip or Microsoft Office to encrypt your files, it's likely that Windows 10 still has one or more temporary copies of unencrypted files hidden on the drive. Other user accounts on your computer will not have access to the files contained in the encrypted folder.

Now that your file or folder is encrypted, you won't need a password to access it other than the password you use to access your Windows profile when you turn on your computer. As long as you are logged into Windows with your account, you will be able to log in and work with encrypted folders or files. If you need to password protect or encrypt the data you use frequently, you need to install a third party program that will allow you to protect your files and folders.

To keep you safe, Microsoft offers built-in file and folder encryption for Windows operating systems. In Microsoft Office Suite, you can use built-in encryption to password protect Office files such as Word documents or

PowerPoint presentations. Microsoft Windows offers a built-in ability to encrypt files and folders on hard drives and removable media using its Encrypting File System. Encrypting Files and Folders with Microsoft Encrypted File System Microsoft EFS offers support for encrypting individual files, folders, and directories on Windows 10 or any version of Windows starting with XP.

You can encrypt individual files, folders, volumes, or entire drives on your computer, as well as flash drives and files stored in the cloud. You can also do this if you only need to encrypt certain files and not the entire computer. When creating a file archive, the content can be encrypted by specifying a password. Open a plain Word document in Microsoft Office, select File, and then select Info.

A window will appear asking if you want to encrypt the selected folder or folder, subfolders and files. Click any letter in the highlighted volume name, click Choose File, and navigate to its parent folder. Double-click the selected drive to open another encrypted container window.

Select Apply Changes to Encryption-Only Folder or Apply Changes to This Folder, Subfolders, and Files, then click OK. Click the pop-up message "Backing up the file encryption key." All subfolders and files within a folder are also encrypted, but if you want to change them, repeat the above process and choose to apply changes only to this folder instead of applying changes to this folder, subfolders and files. Select your preferences and click OK. You can also backup the file's encryption key. Choose a location to save the certificate and name the encryption backup file.

Encrypting folders in Windows XP Professional does not require a password. If you're a Windows 10 Home user, you'll need to encrypt your files with a third-party encryption app. Use a dedicated encryption tool (recommended). If you think Windows 10 encryption tools are not good enough for your files, you can try third-party encryption software.

What you need to know Activate Bitlocker (Windows) or FileVault (Mac) or download an encryption app to protect your files and privacy. Encrypt everything on your computer with a free application like VeraCrypt or TrueCrypt. With support for AES, Serpent, and TwoFish keys, VeraCrypt is a free, cross-platform data protection tool that can encrypt your files any way you want.

YOUR SYSTEM'S SWEETSPOTS: CEO'S ADVICE ON BASIC CYBER SECURITY

AxCrypt is a great free encryption utility that allows users to encrypt all files in a folder and prevent them from being viewed unless the passphrase (password) is known. Free file archiver with high compression and strong AES-256 encryption in 7z and ZIP formats. Password-Protected Folders and Files in Microsoft Windows If you're using Windows 10, you don't need special software to create password-protected hidden folders. In most versions of Windows, files and folders cannot be password protected, so they must be encrypted, or a third-party password protector must be used to protect folders from cybercrime in Windows 7, 8, and 10 .

Cyber Security for Mac Computers

Despite not being pursued by malware authors, users of the Apple OS X platform have been inundated with warnings from analysts, security vendors Symantec, and IT administrators who all believe that a major attack is coming to the Mac. Apple Mac users are strongly advised to update their Apple macOS software now as they are at "serious risk" of hackers exploiting what has been described as one of the biggest hacking vulnerabilities on tech giants' computers in years.

Apple has released security updates for a zero-day vulnerability affecting all iPhones, iPads, Macs, and Apple Watches, a zero-day vulnerability affecting all iPhones, iPads, Macs, and Apple Watches. Apple released security updates for its iPhones, iPads, Apple Watches and Macs that close a vulnerability reportedly exploited by invasive spyware created by NSO Group, an Israeli security company. created by NSO Group, an Israeli security company Invasive spyware created by NSO Group, an Israeli security company NSO Group, an Israeli security company. Apple also released watchOS 7.6.2, macOS Big Sur 11.6, and a security update for macOS Catalina to fix the vulnerability.

An Apple spokesperson confirmed that the latest version of macOS includes fixes for major issues. The iOS 14.7.1 update also fixes a bug that could prevent iPhone Touch ID from unlocking the Apple Watch.

Microsoft is warning Mac users to update to the latest version of macOS Monterey after discovering a vulnerability in the Apple Transparency, Consent and Control (TCC) feature of Apple Transparency, Consent and Control (TCC). Apple's new iPhone OS goes on sale on Monday, but iPhone owners should still update their phones over the weekend before critical security patches can be installed.

Apple thanks Citizen Lab for providing the exploit sample, which Apple says does not pose a threat to most users. `` After discovering the flaw in Apples iMessage Apples iMessage quickly developed and implemented a fix to protect Apple users. The new macOS vulnerability is still valid even if macOS patches similar results above (now tagged as CVE-2020-27937).

When exploited on unpatched systems, the new macOS vulnerability could allow an attacker to potentially launch an attack based on protected user identities. Exploiting a vulnerability in Apples Transparency could allow attackers to spoof Apples Transparency and install malware or hijack another application on your computer. Discovered and reported by Cedric Owens, an offensive security researcher, the bug - a logical fallacy - reportedly allows an attacker to bypass Apple's file quarantine and notary requirements. This particular bug negatively impacts Apple macOS users, especially those who use their own email client such as the Mail app.

Code Execution Errors in Apple macOS Apple macOS allows a remote attacker to execute arbitrary commands on your device. Independent security researcher Park Minchan has discovered a vulnerability in macOS that allows an attacker to execute commands on your computer. We've reached out to Apple to confirm Patrick Wardle's report, and macOS 11.3 includes a fix for this specific vulnerability.

Worst of all, Apple hasn't fully patched it yet, as Ars tested. Apple has found that its products suffer from security flaws, said it was too difficult to patch users running vulnerable and earlier versions of its software, and when it released a security patch to at least some of its at-risk users - because he failed miserably to defend himself against the problem he was supposed to defend. In fact, Apple even forbids access to the App Store with basic features, not to mention the complex features that security companies would like to integrate with them.

By contrast, exploits for known and critical security flaws in the Firefox browser existed for nine days before the Mozilla Foundation released a patch to fix the issue. In October 2009, Microsoft security engineers admitted that the Firefox browser was vulnerable since a security issue discovered in the Windows Presentation Foundation Browser Plugin in February of that year. Since the Firefox browser generally has fewer exposed security vulnerabilities than Microsoft Edge (see Web browser comparison), improved security is often cited as a reason to switch from Internet Explorer to Firefox.

This means malware can bypass all checks performed by Apple's security mechanisms, such as Gatekeeper and File Quarantine, which are designed to prevent malicious apps from running without permission. So presumably this bug allows malware to bypass XProtect. Once confirmed, the malware installation will not be interrupted by the Mac's security tools, although Apple's macOS should stop any changes to critical system files and ask users if the app can access photos, microphone or other systems.

Allowing apps from anywhere, including those from unknown developers, can potentially leave a Mac vulnerable to certain malware and unwanted programs, and should be avoided by all Mac users except those with truly advanced skills. While Mac users don't have to worry about their calculator apps, they should be concerned that supposed PDFs might launch random apps on their computers without causing many alarm bells.

Below is a list of the most common types of malware that threaten Mac computers. The most active malware is Trojan horses or worms, not computer viruses.

1. Ransomware. The worst malware on the block, ransomware takes files or even entire devices hostage. Hackers use ransomware to take over personal or valuable files and demand payment in exchange for the files' decryption.

2. Trojans. A Trojan horse is a kind of malware that finds its way onto your device by pretending to be harmless or even helpful. Meanwhile, in the background, it steals your data or downloads other malware onto the infected device. Mac Trojans often download additional hidden malware to your system like adware or rootkits.

3. Adware. This is a particularly annoying kind of malware that takes over your computer, inundating it with endless ads and pop-ups that can harm your device, track you, and impact performance. Avast blocked 41 million Mac adware threats in 2017 alone, showing that adware is one of the most common types of Mac malware out there.

4. Viruses. A computer virus is a piece of code that hijacks a device's resources without the user's permission. It then replicates itself and spreads across devices and networks, leaving a stream of destruction in its wake. On macOS, viruses are likely hidden in word document files (such as .DOC or .DOCX), and they spring to life as soon as you enable macros.

5. Spyware. Hackers use malicious spying software, or spyware, to gain access to browsing behavior, banking details, keystroke patterns, or other compromising personal information. The information gathered can then be used for identity theft or sold to third parties.

6. Rootkits. Rootkits bury deep into a device, acquiring root access to the machine. While not the most common form of Mac malware, rootkits have

been possible on macOS ever since hackers developed the 2009 Mac-based Machiavelli malware.

7. Phishing. Pis a type of social engineering wherein cybercriminals impersonate a brand or close connection to trick you into revealing sensitive information that can be used for identity fraud or monetary theft.

8. PUPs. Potentially Unwanted Programs usually come bundled with other software you download. From browser toolbars that track your internet history and show you ads to cryptomining programs that can hijack your device's processing power.

"Malware" includes computer viruses and many other forms of malware, such as computer worms, ransomware, spyware, adware, Trojans, keyloggers, rootkits, bootkits, malicious browser helper objects (BHOs), and more. malicious software. For example, viruses and trojans are two specific types of malware, both of which are malware. Computer viruses are a special type of self-replicating malware, such as infectious agents with similar names in humans and animals.

The term "virus" refers to the means of replication, not how malware operates on a computer. Because viruses have historically been the first type of malware to attack personal computers, the security industry often uses the term "antivirus" for software that detects and destroys malware. To help you understand malware, we'll look at the most common terms used to describe malware that can harm your computer and mobile device and compromise your security and privacy.

Malware, short for "malicious software", is used by attackers to intentionally damage and infect devices and networks. A computer worm infiltrates devices through security vulnerabilities, malicious links or files. As soon as users download malicious code to their devices, often delivered through malicious ads or phishing emails, a computer virus spreads to their systems.

Because software is often designed with security features to prevent unauthorized use of system resources, many viruses must exploit and manipulate security bugs, which are security flaws in a system or application software, in order to spread and infect other computers. Many of these viruses can be removed by restarting the computer, entering Microsoft Windows "safe mode" over the network, and then using system tools or the Microsoft Security Scanner. Many users install antivirus software that can detect and eliminate known viruses when the computer tries to download or run an executable file (which might be distributed as an email attachment or on a USB flash drive, for example).

If you want to keep your Mac virus-free, it is recommended that you use antivirus/antimalware software. Free antivirus programs will give you some protection, but paid antivirus programs like Malwarebytes for Mac can detect and block malware before it reaches your Mac. A third-party antivirus application is required. That's all you need to do to keep your Mac completely safe from any Mac OS X malware ever released in the wild.

The only malware in nature that can affect Mac OS X is a few Trojans, which can be easily avoided by practicing computer security (see below). Before you panic, Mac malware and viruses are very rare "in nature". By design, the Mac operating system is more secure against virus and malware threats, but there are many more ways malware can get in.

As cybercriminals become more adept at finding exploits and other vulnerabilities, more and more Macs are falling victim to malware. Virus writers have learned to find backdoors and other vulnerabilities that Macs can also target. Virus and malware creators are ready to attack anyone, including Mac users.

It's well known that Windows computers tend to deal with a range of viruses and malware, but many people don't realize that Mac computers also face similar threats. If you're a Mac user, you get mixed messages about viruses and other malware being a real threat. Get a complete overview of malware terminology, including viruses, worms, spyware, and other dangers that threaten your Mac and your data.

Mac threats include malware such as spyware, keyloggers, backdoors, and more. Remember, while many people use the term "virus" as a reference for any form of malware, most of the digital threats available tend to be various types of malware that can definitely affect a Mac. The fact is that there are a lot of viruses today . less important, especially since there are much easier ways to infect a Mac with Trojans, worms, spyware, and ransomware.

If you're running Windows on a Mac, you should be running Windows Antivirus, which should detect and quarantine/remove any threats. Macs are not immune to malware, but no real virus can run on Mac OS X, and not since Mac OS X was released more than a decade ago. Additionally, OS X is good at preventing unauthorized applications from running, so there are currently no known (self-propagating) malicious viruses or worms targeting OS X. Apple has also implemented an initial malware scanner, XProtect, in OS X, which is being updated to detect malware called MacDefender, and possibly any keylogger malware if it comes along in the future.

Trojans are programs disguised as useful tools that actually contain malware that gets installed on your computer without your knowledge. Trojans provide attackers with backdoor access to devices, perform keylogging, install viruses or worms, and steal data.

This is because Trojans can download all sorts of malware into your system as a gateway, or at least make your computer vulnerable to attacks. Trojans can infect both Macs and PCs and are often introduced through fake software installers or unsecured updates.

Macro viruses - Attack computers by executing code that can take screenshots, format hard drives, corrupt files, deliver more malware, and access webcams and microphones. Viruses can change the functions and applications of a computer; copy, delete and steal data; encrypt data to carry out ransomware attacks; and perform DDoS attacks. A common misconception among Mac users is that Apple computers are immune to viruses and other types of Apple Mac malware (malware).

How Can Mac Computer Users Protect Themselves from Cyber Attacks

Having a Mac antivirus that provides adequate protection is perhaps the single most important thing you can do to protect your Mac. and install a good security program. As described above, Mac users should install antivirus software on their computer in the same way as Windows users. While you can manually remove malware on a Mac, it's best if you have Mac antivirus software installed on your computer.

These security features don't mean your Mac will never be infected with malware. Macs are not as vulnerable as Windows computers, but viruses and hackers can also successfully attack them. Macs can be attacked successfully, and Mac users should never settle for security. According to Kaspersky Lab, the truth is that both Macs and PCs are extremely vulnerable to cyber threats and cyber attacks.

The growing popularity of Mac computers has made them an increasingly attractive target for cybercriminals, and as a result, we are seeing more and more Mac users fall victim to viruses, malware, and cyber threats. In addition to new threats, users of the Apple Mac family of computers are often exposed to risks associated with phishing, spam, and almost any other type of cyber threat. Despite the decline in malware targeting macOS, many Mac users are now realizing they need to be more prepared than ever before. Since active defense is the best defense, Apple's line of Macs may not have significant protection due to infrequent updates.

To some extent, the level of security you will use will depend on the version of macOS or the Microsoft Windows platform you are running. In addition to a strong software and hardware ecosystem, Apple's Mac line of computers has also earned a reputation for being "safer" than Windows PCs. While the popularity of Mac computers can be attributed to their sleek design and ease of use, the lack of persistent malware was probably also interesting. User behavior may be more vulnerable on the Apple Mac line of computers due to perceived relative security compared to the Microsoft Windows platform.

Because Apple hasn't invested the time, energy, or intelligence of Windows into malware prevention and security, Apple is actually making Macs more vulnerable to attack. The point is that while the vast majority of cyber threats still target Windows PCs, corporate devices are not, and never have been, protected from these threats. Even if you turn on all of Apple's security features, it's not enough to keep your Mac 100% safe from the latest malware.

Even with malware attacks on Macs, none of them were big enough to convince Mac users to take preventive action against them. Like PC users for years, Mac users are now taking steps to harden the security of their computers and install anti-malware products. It's critical that Mac users keep their operating system and software up to date, as each update includes fixes to help protect against malicious attacks that Apple knows about.

While more and more Mac users are being targeted by cybercriminals these days, making simple changes like the ones described in this article can help you fully protect your Mac and data from theft. Windows and Mac users are at risk, but these tips will help protect your data and personal information. In just a few simple steps, you can easily protect your Mac and your most important data.

To help you, I will list some of the best security software for your Mac desktop or laptop to help you protect your data and identity online. We hope that the above security software will help you fully secure your Apple macOS products and protect them from the next cyber attack. There are many Mac security threats, from malware to vulnerabilities, and like all operating systems, macOS receives regular updates to address security issues. The first thing a user can do to reduce the risk of cyberattacks, regardless of operating system, is to install an Internet Security software package such as Norton Security (for both Mac and PC) on the computer.

As Mac computers become more popular, users need to learn how to protect themselves in the same way that Windows PC users do. Mac and Windows PC users will claim to have the best operating system (OS), but when it comes to security, there aren't as many differences as you might think. Using a Mac will not protect you from phishing attacks or other web attacks.

Because ransomware uses the user more than the operating system, there are several technical barriers to creating a Mac-targeted attack, as the entry point is to force the user to do something they shouldn't. It is still possible for a Mac user to download an app from an untrusted source, click on a link in a phishing email, or install malware on their computer, unknowingly or otherwise. Hackers may want to steal, change or delete information on your devices and often do so by installing malware (software used for malicious purposes) that you may not even know exists.

The myth that Macs are immune to viruses or attack is dangerous, especially given that Apple's sales figures are strong and the number of active Mac users exceeds 100 million and continues to grow. So far, the most common attack vector for Mac computers has been malware designed to bypass Apple's built-in security tools (Xprotect and Gatekeeper).

Whether you use your Mac for everyday tasks and work projects, or you have a Mac computer system used by multiple employees and users in your organization, it's critical that you properly protect your work Macs.

Mac OS X (Changing the computer name also changes the login address your Mac takes on the local network. If you want to change the computer name of your computer, click the padlock icon at the bottom of the display. Click the padlock to make the change. Next, you can go to Network and Specific Shares checks that you have changed the name of your Apple Mac computer correctly. By default, your Mac will disable any Change button name that changes your computer's name.

For example, if you have device tracking turned on using the Find My iPhone app on your iPhone, your computer name will appear on your iPhone. You can manually change your hostname from Hi ALL. You can also assign a global hostname so that anyone outside your network can find your computer.

Your Mac dynamically assigns a hostname each time the IP address changes. The hosts file on Windows, Name/MacOS or Linux maps hostnames to IP addresses. Each computer that is assigned an IP address on the SCS network must also have a hostname (also known as a computer name).

The MAC address is unique at the hardware manufacturer level, and SCS data centers use these hardware addresses to provide unique access to our network. This may also be referred to as a media access control (MAC) address, a host ID, or a server ID. Use this method to get the MAC address of the local computer and query the computer name or IP address remotely.

You can find your MAC address with the steps above, but finding your computer name is a little different. You can also open Start > Settings > Network and Internet, click on the connection name, then scroll down to see the physical (MAC) address. Under the Ethernet heading, find and write down the physical address. In the Properties box, scroll down, select Locally

Administered Address, and check the Value box; there you will see the MAC addresses of your network cards.

Edit If you have the local IP address of a computer on the network and need to get that computer's name, there is a simple method using the ping command on the Windows command prompt. The -a option of the ping command tells it to resolve the hostname of an IP address, after which it will give you the name of a computer on the network.

If you need to find your IP address, you can also use the Ipconfig command without the following /all and this will tell you the IP address of your device without all the extra information, which can make the process easier. I really need this In name/macOS, to find the IP address or domain name of another device on the network, use the network utility. This must be the same workgroup name used by other computers. When you enter a domain name in a Mac browser and press Enter, the computer will contact the DNS server to find the IP address associated with the domain name. After determining the IP address for a given Mac address, you should still use Resolve-DNSName to resolve it to a hostname.

If you change the hostname of your server, you may also need to update the DNS server for your network, as well as reconfigure user computers. Users who installed profiles from your server can update their Macs to use the new hostname by obtaining and installing new profiles. Updating the host name and local host name using policy To update the host name, computer name, and local host name, you must create a script that includes the new computer name.

Using a Policy to Change Computer Name Requirements To use a policy to change a computer name, you need a Jamf Pro user account with the Create or Update Policies permission. To rename a remote computer to match the manifest name in Jamf Pro, you can use a policy. If the policy sends the manifest before the policy runs, the name reverts to the name of the currently configured managed computer. You can select a file, press Enter and enter a new name,... In addition to changing the MAC address, the free version also allows you to view the IP configuration.

Don't forget to copy and paste the following command into your TextEdit document and change NEW-MAC-NAME to your computer's new name. In addition to the username, your computer will have a computer name that will be used for many purposes. If a computer on your network already has that name, the Mac will automatically add a numeric suffix to the name to distinguish it. Then select System. After setting up an Apple wireless mouse (whether the old Mighty Mouse or the fancy new Magic Mouse), Mac OS X connects the device to the computer you'll be using it on... Change the Mac Bluetooth name.

In such cases it may come in handy to learn how to modify the auto-generated computer and rename it. On a MacBook, you can find it under the "Advanced" section of the network settings panel. If you get a message that your computer is not found, enter its IP address and try again.

None of the tools mentioned in the other answers (arp, ping, hosts) can be used to resolve hostnames without a name entry for the remote Mac in the hosts file or a DNS server on the local or public network. Hostname: The ping command will display the device name, etc. Use the MacOS name/IP address or localhost name in the URL field.

How To Check If Your Computer Has Become a Botnet

A botnet is simply a collection of computers and other Internet-connected devices controlled by an attacker. Technically, any device connected to the Internet can be attacked and connected to a botnet, which means that the potential scale of a botnet attack is quite large. Botnets can infect virtually any device that is directly or wirelessly connected to the Internet. Once devices are infected, botnets are free to access and modify personal information, attack other computers, and commit other crimes.

Malware used by botnets can be secretly installed on your computer. Any computer with malware installed is part of a botnet and can be used alone or in conjunction with other infected devices for malicious purposes.

A botnet is created when Internet-connected devices that are infected with certain malware come together in a network. A botnet can use any Internet-connected device capable of being infected with malware, including Internet of Things (IoT) devices, computers, servers, and even mobile devices.

Botnets are not usually designed to compromise a single computer; they are designed to infect millions of devices. In addition to tools to undermine cryptocurrencies, botnets are also dangerous for businesses and consumers, as they are used to distribute malware, launch attacks on websites, steal personal information and deceive advertisers.

Spam botnets are also used to spread bots in order to attract more computers to the botnet. They are mainly used to send spam, often including malware, to a dizzying amount of every bot.

A botnet is a network of malware-infected devices used to launch coordinated attacks against a single target (such as a DDoS attack) or multiple targets (such as an email phishing attack). Botnets are networks of hijacked computer equipment used to conduct various fraudulent activities and cyberattacks. A botnet is a group of infected devices discovered by hackers and obeying their commands, often including launching attacks on other systems.

A botnet is successful when it can infect a computer without the user's knowledge and spread it to other machines to add it to its network. A botnet is a form of malware that involves an interconnected network of hacked computers that leads back to a centralized computer controlled by a cybercriminal, who can then easily spread cyberattacks throughout the network. Because infected computers are under the control of shepherd bots, a botnet is like a malicious hacker inside your network, not just a malicious executable.

Usually a robotic machine (the computer has been infected with malware, the attackers who control the botnet are called "shepherd bots"). Mainly due to malware infection. The term botnet is actually an acronym for "robot network" and refers to a group of bots (computers, cell phones, IoT devices) that are now under the control of bots that are part of a machine attack. (computers, mobile phones, IoT devices).

The goal of a botnet is to infect as many connected devices as possible and use the computing power and scalability of those devices to perform automated actions that would normally remain hidden from device users. Regardless of the reason, botnets end up being used for all sorts of attacks, both on users controlled by the botnet and on other people. Cybercriminals love botnets because botnets give criminals control over thousands of computers at once and help hide the identity of cybercriminals.

Cybercriminals can use the combined processing power of botnets to carry out fraudulent schemes. The most dangerous spam botnets can run phishing campaigns, spread malware, distribute more bots, and steal sensitive information. Botnets can be used to perform distributed denial-of-service (DDoS) attacks, steal data, [1] send spam, and give an attacker access to a device and its connection.

These computers can then be used by criminal hackers to send spam or launch DDOS attacks, in which botnet bots are instructed to send large volumes of communication requests to the target system. Criminal hackers can also use these bots to collect data, as they can install spyware on your computer to track keystrokes, collect data continuously, use the system to monitor its network, or as a starting point for other attacks. other bots. Malware can use digital signatures, so only someone with access to the private key can control the botnet.

Botnets can be used to distribute malware, such as viruses, to take control of a normal user's computer/software.[33] By taking control of someone's personal computer, they have unlimited access to their personal information, including passwords and account login information. Botnets can be used to monitor network traffic, either passively to collect information and steal credentials, or to actively inject malicious code into HTTP traffic. Botnets can infect and use laptops, desktops, servers, routers, smartphones, or any other network equipment to perform malicious activities.

Botnets use P2P networks and file sharing services to infect computers. Botnets are typically computer networks infected with malware (computer viruses, keyloggers, and other malicious software) and remotely controlled by cybercriminals, usually for profit or to carry out attacks on websites or networks. In order for your computer to become part of a botnet, it must first be infected with malware that communicates with a remote server or other infected computer on the network in order to receive instructions from whoever controls the botnet, which is usually hackers and criminals.

A botnet attack can consist of hundreds or even more than a million infected devices, each running malicious code on behalf of a bot owner. Nearly all Internet computer devices are vulnerable to a botnet, which means that the threat is constantly growing. A person who manages the command and control infrastructure, a bot shepherd or botmaster, uses compromised computers or bots to launch attacks aimed at disrupting the target network, injecting malware, harvesting credentials, or performing high-intensity CPU activities.

There are many different methods you can use to determine if your computer has been attacked by a botnet. There is a simple reason why anomaly detection can detect infected systems that are not part of a botnet.

Smart devices such as computers, cell phones and IP cameras are at risk of being infected and becoming part of a botnet. A botnet can use any Internet-connected device capable of being infected with malware, including Internet of Things (IoT) devices, computers, servers, and even mobile devices. A botnet is created when Internet-connected devices that are infected with certain malware come together in a network. Botnets are computer networks infected with malware and used to commit cybercrime.

Botnets are networks of computers infected with malware that allow them to be controlled remotely. A botnet is a network of infected computers, controlled by a single host and working together to achieve a goal. A botnet is a network of infected computers or other networked devices that communicate with each other to perform the same malicious activities, such as launching spam campaigns or distributed denial of service attacks. A botnet is successful when it can infect a computer without the user's knowledge and spread it to other machines to add it to its network.

It is simply a set of bots on compromised computers and devices that execute commands given by the botnet owner to the botnet owner. His job is to find vulnerable devices and their advantages for the development of a botnet. This use could also be used to increase the size of botnets by attacking multiple devices, or perhaps going idle and simply harvesting data from millions of infected devices. The term botnet alludes to the fact that the purpose of this activity is to infect as many machines as possible in order to add them to your network to perform illegal activities in large numbers.

In order for your computer to be part of a botnet, it must first be infected with malware that communicates with remote servers or other infected computers on the network in order to receive instructions from those who control the botnet, usually hackers and criminals. A botnet is a group of infected devices discovered by hackers and obeying their commands, often including launching attacks on other systems. A botnet is a network of malware-infected devices used to launch coordinated attacks against a single target (such as a DDoS attack) or multiple targets (such as an email phishing attack). A botnet consists of a collection of interconnected computers and devices that can be captured and controlled for cyberattacks.

Botnets can also be used by anyone who can muster such an army of computers, but they are often run by organized online criminal groups to commit fraud. Spam botnets are primarily used to send spam messages, often with malware, in dizzying numbers of each bot, and to spread the bots to attract more computers to the botnet. Some botnets are used to steal information, while others are used to send spam. Botnets are commonly used for DDoS attacks and can also leverage their collective computing power to send mass spam, steal credentials on a massive scale, or spy on people and organizations.

While hackers can infiltrate your device through botnets, they can also use entire botnet armies to disrupt your website or online activity. Once a botnet is created, hackers can control it in a number of ways. It may seem simple and almost harmless, but as the previous paragraph demonstrated, it's a powerful site behind some of the worst attacks a hacker can attempt. Literally, "Bot" is short for "robot," and adding "network" creates a "botnet," which means "network of bots"; and hackers who control other people's computers are called "robot shepherds."

The bot is similar to a traditional Trojan horse; but instead of just installing a keylogger or password thief (which it could still do), the bot works with other infected PCs, making them all act together, sort of like a very large computer. A botnet usually consists of hundreds or even millions of devices, including PCs, Macs, Linux servers, home routers, smartphones, etc. Computers are the main devices in a botnet, and the malware that infects them is injected from a phishing email, a website or click fraud campaigns. Botnets can infect computers, laptops, servers, smartphones, and all kinds of IoT devices with security vulnerabilities.

Another way botnets infiltrate your systems is to look for insecure devices, from baby monitors to computers, and access insecure devices with weak passwords. Detecting botnets can be difficult because hackers have an interest in making sure that victims don't know their devices are infected. Using information obtained from the Simda botnet control servers, Kaspersky Lab has created a special page where you can check if your computer's IP address is on the infected list.

While the Simda botnet has been suspended, people whose computers are infected should get rid of this malware as soon as possible. The Simda botnet is a commercial botnet used to distribute illicit software and various types of malware, including malware capable of stealing financial credentials.

Coordinated Internet attacks are used to increase the size of a botnet and attack more devices, and to collect data from millions of infected devices. Botnets allow viruses to reach as many people as possible in a short period of time, especially if they try to infect devices via email or over an open network. Instead of being hit by a zombie botnet you may never have seen, you can spend a few minutes a week looking at what botnets have been identified and named by security experts.

One often overlooked way to prevent a computer from becoming part of a botnet is to use a web filtering solution. To prevent a computer from joining a botnet, you need to use technological controls and apply best security practices.

It is much easier to prevent a computer from falling into a botnet than it is to detect a malware infection and fix it after it is installed. Malicious software used by botnets can be secretly installed on your computer. Any computer on which malware is installed is part of a botnet and can be used alone or in conjunction with other compromised devices for malicious purposes. These botnets are used to attack (and often infect) other computers and devices.

Botnets are also dangerous for businesses and consumers as they are used to spread malware, launch attacks on websites, steal personal information, and deceive advertisers. Spam botnets are primarily used to send spam messages, often with malware, in dizzying numbers by each bot, and to spread bots to attract more computers to the botnet. When cybercriminals themselves inject malware into collective device control botnets, they are used to carry out cyberattacks. Botnets are not usually designed to compromise a single computer; they are designed to infect millions of devices.

Once devices are infected, botnets are free to access and modify personal information, attack other computers, and commit other crimes. To create a botnet, hackers start by creating malware (or getting ready-to-use malware that can be modified) that can be used to remotely control a host computer or other infected device.

To take over your computer for use in a botnet, a hacker can install malware on it. You need to determine if your computer is part of a botnet, remove the daemon, and then install blocks that keep malware away from your device. If your antivirus software has detected malware on your computer, your computer may be part of a botnet.

Reliable antivirus software will stop most botnet malware from being installed on your computer, and if you've already been infected, you can usually remove them easily. Taking simple, common-sense precautions when using the internet can not only remove installed botnets, but also prevent them from being installed on your computer, tablet, and phone in the first place.

Sometimes even the best precautions can be overcome by a botnet attack, by the time you discover them on the network before it's too late. As different types of devices become available, often with their own security settings, it is difficult to track, monitor and stop these attacks before they happen.

By learning more about how a botnet works and implementing appropriate measures on your network, you can ensure that your system is protected from such threats. While it's impossible to magically protect yourself from botnet operators, you can increase your chances of not becoming a part of them by following the same common sense strategies you should use to avoid all computer viruses. By now, it should be clear that preventing botnet infection requires a comprehensive strategy; one that includes good browsing habits and antivirus protection.

Fortunately, certain services will help you identify botnet activity on your computer. You may never notice that your computer is part of a botnet used to relay spam because botnets are not that big. Worst of all, your computer can be recruited into a botnet as easily as 1-2-3.

Preventing botnets from using your computer or device is relatively simple. A botnet is simply a collection of computers and other networked devices controlled by an attacker. DDoS attacks typically use botnets, which are computers or other devices that are infected with malware and controlled by hackers. There are many different types of DDoS attacks, but hackers typically use botnets to send large amounts of web traffic or requests to websites, applications, or servers.

A botnet is a network of malware-infected devices used to launch coordinated attacks against a single target (such as a DDoS attack) or multiple targets (such as an email phishing attack). A hacker or attacker can then remotely control all the computers in the botnet as a group to perform actions such as sending spam, conducting DDoS attacks, creating fake network traffic, serving ads to all botnet members, or forcing users to delete payments. from a botnet. Cybercriminals love botnets because botnets allow criminals to control thousands of computers simultaneously and help hide the identities of cybercriminals. Botnets are also used to find new vulnerable devices and infect them with other Trojans, viruses, and, of course, special malware that brings them into botnets.

Botnets can infect and use laptops, desktops, servers, routers, smartphones, or any other network equipment to perform malicious activities. Botnets are typically computer networks infected with malware (computer viruses, keyloggers, and other malicious software) and remotely controlled by cybercriminals, usually for profit or to carry out attacks on websites or networks. Computers are the main devices in a botnet, and the malware that infects them comes from a phishing email, a hacked website, or a click fraud campaign. Computers are most commonly targeted by botnets through malware sent through spam email campaigns, such as those sent by these two spam botnets.

The best way to remove it is to run a virus scan on your computer, which should detect botnet malware and then remove it for you - a simple solution to a serious problem.

How to Tell If Your Computer is Infected with Rootkit

Rootkits are a malware software programs that provide the attacker illegal access to the target computer system and control the target computer system. Although Rootkits have been in existence since the first days of the calculation, they have developed significantly in recent years and have become an increasingly prevailing threat to both organizations and individuals. This essay will provide a comprehensive Rootkits review, including their history, characteristics, types, detection methods and softening strategies.

For the first time in the early 1990s, the term "rootkit" created by a hacker named "Stormbringer, was created for the first time. At that time, Rootkits were primarily used by attackers to fully control unix -based systems. Since then, Rootkits has evolved and developed significantly and developed significantly evolving and developing significantly, and Rootkits developed significantly and developed significantly evolving and developing significantly evolving and developing significantly evolving and developing significantly evolving and developing significantly evolving and developing significantly. Rootkits also evolved and developed significantly and developed significantly and developed significantly. It is now possible to find on almost any computing platform, including Windows, Mac OS and Linux.

One of the most significant features of Rootkits is their ability to disguise their presence from the operating system and safety software. Rootkits do this by modifying system files or nuclear code to hide their presence and prevent detection. Rootkits can also use a variety of methods to avoid detection, such as logging in to system calls or using encryption to contact the attacker's team and control server.

There are several different types of rootkits, including user mode rootkits, nuclear mode rootkits, hypervaristic Rootkits and bootkits. The user mode Rootkits operates at the program level and can be easily removed. The nuclear mode rootkits work at the system level and are more difficult to detect and remove. Hypervisor level Rootkits operates at the virtual machine level and operates at the boot sector level at the boot sector level.

Rootkits detection can be complicated as they are designed to avoid traditional antiviral and anti-doctrine tools. The most effective way to detect Rootkits is to use a special Rootkit scanner or forensic tool that scans the system memory, file system and any anomalies register. Another way is to analyze system behavior by monitoring network flow and system resources.

The best way to protect yourself from the roots is primarily preventing them from infecting the system. This can be achieved by continuously updating the system software using strong passwords and avoiding suspicious websites and email. Postplapses. Another effective mitigation strategy is to use antivirus and anti-Kalin software software that is specifically designed to detect and remove rootkits.

Rootkits pose a major threat to computer security and can cause significant damage to both organizations and individuals. To determine and prevent these insidious threats, it is necessary to understand the history, characteristics, types, detection methods and reduction strategies associated with Rootkits. By installing effective security measures and vigilant, computer users can protect themselves from the damage caused by these harmful programs.

In today's technological era, computers play a vital role in our daily lives. We use them for many goals such as banking, shopping, communication and more. However, as the use of computers increases, the risk of cyber attacks increased. One of the most dangerous types of cyber attacks is Rootkit infection. This can do great damage to your computer and privacy. Therefore, it is very important to know what to do if your computer is infected with Rootkit. In this essay we will discuss how to detect and remove Rootkit infection from your computer.

First, it is very important to understand what Rootkit is. Rootkit is a type of malware designed to hide yourself and other harmful software from the operating system and safety software. This allows the attacker to obtain illegal access to your computer and steal public information such as passwords, credit card data and other confidential data. Rootkits can also allow the attackers remotely control your computer without your knowledge.

The first step of Rootkit infection detection is to use reliable antivirus software. After installing a reliable antivirus program, run the entire system scan. Antivirus software will detect any malicious program and root sets on your computer. If the antiviral Rootkit detects Rootkit, it will encourage it to be removed. Follow the instructions carefully.

Manual root sets can be heavy because they are designed to hide. However, you can use Rootkit to use the usefulness of Microsoft called Rootkit Deadle, Rootkit. This utility can detect and distinguish all sets of your system. However, you can be careful using this program as it can sometimes mislead the legitimate system files as Rootkits.

Removing Rootkit from a computer can be a difficult task. In some cases, Rootkit can only be removed by reinstalling the operating system. This can be a time -consuming process and you can lose all your data if you have supported it in advance. However, if you have a recent backup, you can restore files and operating system in a pre -infected state.

Another option is to use a specialized Rootkit removal tool. These tools are designed to detect and remove root sets from your system. Some popular Rootkit removal tools are Avast, Kaspersky and Malwwarebytes.

Rootkit infection is a major threat to your computer and privacy. If you suspect your computer has been infected with Rootkit, the first step is to do all the system scanning using reliable antivirus software. If the scan determines Rootkit, carefully follow the instructions provided by the antivirus software. Alternatively, you can use a specialized Rootkit removal tool to remove it. If everything else fails, you may need to reinstall your operating system. Therefore, it is necessary to maintain regular backups for your important data to prevent data loss. Finally, prevention is the best attitude.

Memory dump analysis is an essential process that ensures PCS infected with root sets. Rootkits can hide its presence in the system by modifying the operating system behavior and hiding their activities. These harmful programs are a major threat to the safety and privacy of personal and business computer systems.

The process of memory dumpanalysis includes extraction and examination and examination of RAM from the computer. In simple terms, it is like a instant image of a computer memory at a given time of time. Information in the memory dumpcan help you analyze your computer's activities, including Rootkits.

In order to secure a computer infected with Rootkit, memory dump analysis is vital to determine the malware responsible for the violation. Memory dump analysis can provide insight into Rootkit activities such as the files it has achieved, the changes he has made for the system, and any connection it had with other systems. This knowledge is necessary to determine the source of the infection, the extent of the damage and the actions that need to be taken to remove the root from the system.

Memory dump analysis is a complex process that requires specialized skills and tools. Analysis includes examination of a memory dump analysis to determine patterns or abnormalities that could show the presence of the root. Analysis tools can be used to scan the known Rootkit signature landfill or set a harmful code that would be injected into legitimate system processes.

Another step in the process includes analysis of the behavior of identified Rootkit to understand its tactics, methods and procedures. This step can reveal the goal of Rootkit, its capabilities and communication channels. By understanding this information, analysts can design responsibility to detect and prevent similar root sets to infect the system in the future.

The memory dump analysis is a critical process to secure a computer infected with Rootkit. It is a complex process that requires specialized measures and competence to determine the main cause of infection, responsible malware and actions needed to remove the root from the system. As an analysis of the memory landfill, analysts can acquire valuable insights into Rootkit behavior, design contradictions to prevent malicious programs and prevent future infections. memory dumpanalysis is a powerful tool that can help protect personal and business computer systems from malicious roots.

In today's digital age, cyber threats have become more common, and cybercriminals use advanced methods to penetrate computer systems. Rootkit is one of these types of malicious software designed to hide its presence from victim and prevent detection by safety software. Rootkit operates the operating system and can provide the attacker access to the computer system, causing data theft, destruction or manipulation. Memory forensic analysis is an effective technique to protect a computer infected with Rootkit malware.

Memory Forensic Analysis is a process of a volatile computer system memory analysis to extract useful information about running processes, files and network connections. An unstable memory captures temporary data created by the operating system and programs, including the Rootkit malware.

Memory forensic analysis can provide insight into Rootkit behavior and methods that attackers use to bypass antiviral and other security measures.

The first step in memory forensic analysis is the acquisition of a memory landfill, which is a copy of the computer memory during the attack. This can be done using a variety of tools such as FTK Imager and volatility. Once the memory landfill is purchased, it can be analyzed using memory forensic tools such as variability system and GRANDAL. These tools can reveal the presence of Rootkit, its files and network activities.

Memory forensic analysis can reveal Rootkit behavior, such as its durability mechanism and methods used to hide its presence. For example, Rootkit could be hooked to the nucleus to hide its files or injected its code into legitimate processes to prevent detection. Memory forensic analysis can also reveal Rootkit communications channels such as network connections and data that Rootkit sends or receives.

Rootkit behavioral and communication channels can be taken on the basis of the results of the analysis can be taken with appropriate mitigation measures. For example, the system can be distinguished from the network to prevent further data theft or destruction. Rootkit files can be recognized and removed, and system configurations can be restored in the previous state.

Memory forensic analysis is the main technique to protect computers infected with Rootkit malware. This provides insight into the Rootkit behavioral and communication channels and help to determine the necessary mitigation measures to prevent further damage. Organizations had to teach specialists to carry out memory forensic analysis and should regularly review and update their security measures to avoid possible cyber attacks.

Part Two: The Fastest Way a Hacker Hacks into Your System CMS

How do Hackers PWN Their Victims

Hackers are capable to divert cookies from websites utilizing malicious code, numerous codes and methods. The malicious rule can be used to path consumer's actions when they login into a website or electronic mail report. Cookies supply an smooth way for hackers to attain as they store the attestations of the consumer on the computer. Hackers use cross-home create writing attacks to exploit biscuits and steal impressionable facts. They can therefore use this data for malicious endeavors in the way that taking control of reports, forging new site admin accounts or theft services from system where banking transactions are completed electronically accounts.

Hacking site logins and electronic mail logins from biscuits is a common habit for hackers and cybercriminals to attain to individual data, poster analyses, and abundant services. The first brute force approach secondhand by hackers search out attempt a a lot of username and password alliances as far as individual works. Another order secondhand by hackers is theft stored gathering biscuits from additional users' ploys. This admits bureaucracy to bypass freedom questions and login into the site accompanying stolen attestations.

How do hackers pwn site logins and electronic mail logins from cookies? Cybercriminals use a sort of plans to attain to user reports. One of ultimate average hold a meeting hijacking, which includes communicable control of a consumer's session while they are record into their connected to the internet report. Through this method, cybercriminals can exploit consumers gatherings in consideration of gain access to their passwords and added facts stocked in the website's biscuits. This contains hash passwords, which maybe decrypted by way of specific exploitation forms. Additionally, cybercriminals can again install supplementary malware upon consumers' browsers so that bypass protection measures and abduct some passwords that have been preserved on their gateway. In few cases, hackers may even able to have or do attain outside requiring a login by any means by misusing exposures in the website or by utilizing phishing methods on gullible users the one visit the ground.

The most ordinary method of hack into site logins and electronic mail logins is through password confirmation. A consumer's identification is stored in either ordinary readable form or hash form and the technician can before use the data gap to attain to duties. By using methods in the way that meeting hijacking, attackers can intercept a consumers' gathering tokens and avoid the login process entirely. Furthermore, if an computer software for basic operation has happened endangered, it may be attainable for a technician to attain to passwords that were used on added websites or aids. Hackers can use a sort of tactics to pwn site logins and electronic mail logins from wafers. One way is through small detecting, that allows the technician to monitor site traffic and interrupt login pages. They can therefore use these login pages to steal passwords, usernames, and different delicate dossier. Additionally, if a website has automobile-login authorized or uses feeble TLS encryption, hackers can easily approach this facts also. Another common plan is for hackers to exploit public Wi-Fi networks by detecting the encrypted traffic 'tween users and websites. They can before divert gathering cookies that are secondhand for confirmation purposes or even passwords that were transfer data from one computer system to another on the page itself.

This is usually accomplished by discharge a malicious link to unsuspecting consumers, that when clicked, can establish malware on their calculating that can control or record their browser gathering. The aggressor before has access to the consumer logs and the gathering ID guide their account.

Innocent targets are subjected to a variety of attacks, including credential stuffing, password sprinkling, and fake login pages. Hackers who practice "password spraying" do so in the hopes that some of the accounts they target will have weak passwords. Credential stuffing is the practice of hackers using previously stolen login information from one website to access different online accounts. Cybercriminals can access victims' online accounts and use their personal information for malicious purposes by tricking them into entering their login information on a fake login page. By sending links to unwary recipients that take them to a malicious website and ask them to enter their username and password, they can also carry out credential stuffing attacks.

The hacker will have access to the user's account if they enter their login credentials and can use that information to access other online accounts. Hackers can also guess user passwords or use sophisticated password cracking software to decipher them. With the aid of this software, they can quickly and easily break a password and gain access to the account. Data breaches are another way hackers can take over email and website logins.

Hackers can access login information for other people through data breaches. Data breaches are frequently brought on by people using well-known passwords or weak password complexity. Hackers will use brute force attacks to attempt to crack the password. Hackers use a brute force attack to try to guess the password.

To gain access, hackers attempt as many passwords and password combinations as they can. These passwords are frequently created from most dictionaries and typically contain the most popular passwords. Even some random character combinations that are not in the dictionary but might still contain customized settings from earlier hacks are used by some hackers. The hacker would then have access to the target website's login information. Hackers use test lists, hacking programs, and lists of words that include words from most dictionaries as well as random character combinations and many other unique configurations.

Additionally, they inject malicious code into websites using programs and scripts, exposing your login information. These email password combinations and other credentials can be used by cybercriminals to try credential stuffing techniques on other websites.

Using different passwords for each account and unique, complex passwords overall is the best way to protect your accounts. A minimum of 15 characters must be included in each password, with a combination of capital and lowercase letters, numbers, and symbols. If you have an old email password and use the same password for several accounts, be sure to change them. Data breaches may become more frequent if multiple accounts are compromised. Make it even harder for hackers to access your accounts by using tools like multi-factor authentication and two-factor authentication. This will prevent fraudsters from gaining entry.

Hackers frequently use fake login pages to target people who might have weak passwords. This implies that the hacker has the ability to modify your password and take over your account. Traditional phishing emails are another popular theft technique. The links in these emails direct users to a page where they must enter their actual login names and passwords when they click them. Sending emails with such links and asking recipients to change their passwords or provide their login names and passwords is the most popular method of stealing account information. It's critical to be knowledgeable about these techniques and watchful when it comes to safeguarding your accounts.

If your password is weak, hackers can frequently guess it or "pwn" your email and website logins using a variety of methods. If you use shared computers, someone else could gain access to your accounts through phishing scams used by cybercriminals. When accounts are hacked, frequently unanticipated consequences can happen, making it extremely difficult for people to reset their account.

Hackers employ a variety of methods to take over email and website logins. Hackers frequently employ techniques such as password guessing, password cracking with specialized tools, and password theft from other sources. Additionally, some hackers sell or use video tutorials to show them how to crack email passwords and gain access to another person's email account.

When hackers gain access to your PC or LAN or LAN, they can easily attack your website resulting in WordPress site being hacked or hacked. Hackers can access protected files and damage the protected information of site visitors or apply additional hacks such as SEO spam and phishing. Once they have used malware to gain access to, for example, customer contact information, they can disguise themselves and send thousands of emails to your website users posing as another brand or service. Or WordPress hackers can use a username with a weak password to hack into your site.

Cybercriminals often use "brute force attacks," bombarding user accounts with various password and login combinations in an attempt to guess the correct password. Hackers do the theft by tricking users into installing malware (software designed to cause harm) that copies and sends authentication codes to the hackers.

Once a hacker gets into your site, he can use it to do all sorts of nefarious things. Hackers can scrutinize your code looking for security vulnerabilities that allow them to take control of your website using any platform or script vulnerability. Hackers find a way to inject malicious JavaScript code into your pages, which can then infect the devices of all website visitors exposed to the code. Hackers can insert malware files into files on legitimate websites or inject code into existing files to steal information from websites and their visitors, attempt to gain unauthorized access through backdoor files, or cause general damage.

How to Protect Website CMS Link

Web developers should avoid using "/admin" as CMS URL Slug because hackers can use search engines to locate the CMS URL. This is especially true for popular tools like phpMyAdmin and Wordpress login page. If a malicious attacker is able to find the login URL of these tools, they can easily gain access to the website. To secure sites from these bad guys, it's important that web developers make sure all their url settings are not publicly accessible.

By using a custom slug like '/admin', hackers can easily use search engines to locate the CMS URL, which leads them directly to the login page. To further protect a website and its content, web developers should avoid using default login urls such as 'wp-login.php' or 'wp-admin'. The details of these common login urls are public knowledge and are available online for malicious bots and hackers to use in their attacks against WordPress blogs or other sites running PHP scripts and pages. If possible, it's best to rename the default login url since this will make it harder for hackers to find your site's admin pages. Additionally, passwords should be complex enough that they cannot be easily guessed or brute forced by automated hacking tools.

Web developers should avoid using the "/admin" slug for their CMS URL as it makes it easy for malicious users to locate the login page of sites. Hackers can use search engines to quickly locate a WordPress login page with this slug, making it easier for them to carry out attacks. Not only is the "/admin" slug used by many hackers but also many random bots that are designed to scan websites and try random login attempts with default usernames and passwords. This means that if a WordPress site uses this URL slug, attackers are more likely to identify the login page and try force attacks on it using automated tools. To protect against such attacks, web developers should always follow best practices when setting up a WordPress site. This includes changing the default URL slug from "/admin", enabling two-factor authentication (2FA) on their sites, and installing security plugins like WordFence or iThemes Security Pro.

Web developers should avoid using "/admin" as a CMS URL slug because it can be used by hackers to easily locate the CMS login page. This is especially true for popular content management systems like WordPress. It is a standard login URL and attackers can use search engines to find default login pages.

Furthermore, popular plugins like WP-Login are vulnerable to attacks, making it easier for attackers to gain access. To ensure that web hosts are more secure, they should opt for custom logins or hide their login screens instead of relying on the default "/admin" slug. Additionally, all WordPress vulnerabilities should be patched and monitored regularly, including the WordPress dashboard (wp-admin). By avoiding the "/admin" slug and taking other security measures such as two-factor authentication and security plugins, web developers can increase the level of protection on their websites against potential attackers.

Hackers usually use brute force attacks, applied social science, and program exposures to attain to websites. One way to cover your site search out use parameterized queries. - This helps to prevent hackers from win approach. Another habit is to guarantee you have a secure login whole and use passwords that are troublesome to guess. Hackers can also attain by difficult common passwords or using identification alternator finishes. They can even attempt to use brute force attacks, that includes bothersome different blends of usernames and passwords as far as they infiltrate. Software vulnerabilities are another habit hackers attain, so confirm you have the latest protection revises equipped on your website.

A username and password identification combination is ultimate prevailing way hackers attain to a site's CMS. They can try various passwords and combinations, even utilizing passwords they experience the consumer would use. The hacker will too try to guess the potential username of a believable station user and therefore use that to get the attacker's desired facts. If a profitable SQL dose attack is working, an attacker keep attain to your site's user report. Guessing methods in the way that brute force attacks, or bothersome all likely blends of characters, are another pattern secondhand by attackers to try and acquire approach.

Attackers may likewise use dictionary attacks, that are attempts to guess passwords by a list of commonly used passwords. They can also abduct passwords by utilizing keyloggers or malicious software that records keystrokes. Hackers concede possibility again introduce malware into websites or use SQL injection hacks to attain. A operator can introduce malicious JavaScript into your website and embezzle facts from your consumers. This is known as cross-ground or music (XSS). The aggressor can change page content, redirect guests to different websites, or even keep personal news from the gateway.

Another plan used by hackers is applied social science, place they maneuver your consumers into giving bureaucracy approach to impressionable information.

They ability use phishing attacks to receive your consumers to give out their attestations, or they take care of please malicious links that can contaminate their calculating accompanying malware. They can also study your site's beginning rule, looking for defect in your attendant protection or platform freedom exposures. Another habit hackers gain access to your site is by misusing floor weaknesses in the program they are utilizing.

Hackers frequently use grown website hack methods to attain to CMS Urls and use automated bots to find websites. They can again kidnap your gateway cookie or poison your DNS cache. This admits hackers to control your site foreigners, take control of the browser, and even introduce malicious law into the site artwork. Systems like content administration structure (CMS) are exposed targets for hackers on account of their cross-body exposures. By exploiting these proneness, hackers can attain to delicate information stocked in the databases of the site or system. Additionally, they can use your DNS cache or added methods to poison technician code into the spot or music. This admits ruling class to control browsers and execute malicious rule on wholes that may have happened gave in by distressing websites or other malicious performers.

Software hacking tools provide a comprehensive set of security tools to locate website vulnerabilities and CMS URL. These tools are used for information gathering, searching for common web application vulnerabilities, web application vulnerability scanner, server configuration issues and custom tool development. All these activities help in finding out the weak spots on any website or CMS system. With the use of a vulnerability scanner, hackers can easily uncover any weaknesses in the infrastructure of web applications and servers. This helps them to know where their attack should be focused and how to exploit it.

Web application security is very important and hackers use softwares to locate website vulnerabilities and CMS URL. These softwares are called Security Scanners, which search the web for websites with known security vulnerabilities. The scanner identifies security issues by fingerprinting the web applications and searching for common vulnerabilities. Attackers use this software to identify vulnerable web applications, which allows them to gain access and exploit it.

Ethical hackers, also known as penetration testers, use it to identify security flaws and potential attack vectors. Server scanning tool is a great way for potential attackers to locate specific website vulnerabilities and CMS URL's. Nikto allows penetration testers to analyze a full web server in order to identify any potential attack vectors. Good recon can be done by using this software, which allows the attackers to gain more information about the target system. It can provide detailed information about open ports, HTTP headers, operating systems and other important details that could help an attacker gain access into a system.

A website vulnerability scanner is a piece of software that can be used to identify many different types of vulnerabilities on several web servers. Web scanners are the most commonly used tools in the hacking community, they can scan many different web applications and websites for known vulnerabilities. It can also detect insecure HTTP cookies settings and other misconfigured server software which could lead to many vulnerabilities. Server scanners are used by hackers to locate any potential flaws in a company's server that could lead to an attack or unauthorized access.

These tools can scan for vulnerabilities including SQL injection, web application vulnerabilities, authentication pages, weak password strength and many others. File inclusion and header injection can also be detected by these scanners. Additionally, some of the scanners are able to detect arbitrary file creation which is a common way for hackers to gain access. There are over 200 kinds of known web applications that have been discovered that have security flaws which allow a hacker to gain access through site scripting or sql injection.

To locate these security vulnerabilities, hackers use softwares like Zed Attack Proxy (ZAP) to scan websites and web applications for weaknesses. ZAP is one of the most popular tools used by ethical hackers as it provides detailed information on security flaws and fix recommendations. In addition to ZAP, there are four other popular CMS that can be used to identify potential attack points and vulnerabilities - Appscan, Burp Scanner, Nessus and Web Inspector.

These tools can be used to scan http cookies, web applications, wireless attacks and html5 local storage. Kali Linux is also a popular tool among hackers as it provides numerous security and forensic tools as well as exploitation tools that can be used to locate website vulnerabilities. Furthermore, vulnerability analysis and privacy issues can also be addressed with the use of these softwares.

Each CMS is different in terms of functionality and internal security, but there are some general aspects that need to be taken into account in order to protect them. If you are looking for the most secure CMS solution, Custom CMS is the safe choice. Everyone loves these features, but keeping the CMS as simple as possible, with the exception of security-focused or backup-focused plug-ins, reduces the chance of security issues. If you have built your website with a content management system (CMS), you can enhance your website with security plug-ins that actively prevent website hacking attempts.

Fortunately, many CMSs provide out-of-the-box user management with many of these website security features built in, although some additional configurations or modules may be required to use salted passwords (prior to Drupal 7) or to set the minimum security. password. Please note that some CMS may come pre-configured for maximum security. There are always new security threats, so it's important that you get the essentials before choosing advanced security configurations for your website.

For websites that require even more security, there are specialized vulnerability scanners and application firewalls worth looking into. You can also use security tools and scanners (such as SiteCheck) to look for indicators of compromise or vulnerability. You can't check them manually, but you can scan them all for CMS vulnerabilities with the automatic website malware scanner. To prevent malware, the website scanner must also be able to automatically apply security patches and updates.

Hackers can scrutinize your code for security holes, allowing them to take control of your website using any platform or scripting vulnerability. Website hijackers will make sure they are aware of the latest vulnerabilities and look for any sites that have not been patched.

These are the vulnerabilities that the website can be easily hacked, however, if we design the website with strong security practices, it will be more reliable and less likely to be hacked. Because most websites rely on dozens of different applications, millions of lines of code, and thousands of individual developers (not including your website code itself), we can assume that every operating system, web server, CMS, and website There are loopholes. .Vulnerabilities are basically bugs in website code or security holes in core CMS code or integration of third-party plugins/extensions that allow attackers to penetrate and exploit these vulnerabilities to eventually illegally access sensitive information on your website or inject various malware These attackers completely took over the site and caused a possible data leak. Most website security breaches don't involve stealing your data or changing a website's layout, but rather trying to use your server as an email relay for spam or setting up a temporary web server, often used to serve illegal files.

Most CMS offer security plugins so you can increase the security of your site. If you have built your website with a content management system (CMS), you can enhance your website with security plug-ins that actively prevent website hacking attempts. To protect your website from hacking, always keep an eye on so that your application management system and all scripts you have installed are up to date. Keeping the platform and scripts you have installed up to date is probably one of the best things you can do to protect your site from any security breaches.

Good site management will not eliminate risk, your site will never be 100% secure, but by carefully maintaining and following best practices, you can reduce the chances of your site being hacked while still maintaining a great user experience. A poorly secured website can put your device and data, as well as your customers and visitors, at risk. Threats to your website security can harm not only you and your business, but your audience as well. You might think there's nothing worth hacking on your site, but sites are always under attack.

When website security flaws are found in the software, hackers are quick to try to exploit them. Hackers find a way to inject malicious JavaScript code into your pages, which can then infect the devices of all website visitors exposed to the code.

Once malicious PHP code is uploaded to your site, hackers can execute it and take effective control of your site. Hackers can scrutinize your code for security holes, allowing them to take control of your website using any platform or scripting vulnerability. Before we move on to discussing ways to secure a CMS, we can list the ways in which a hacker can take control of a website.

There is a combination of factors that make a CMS vulnerable to hacker attacks. As the most popular CMS platform hosting over 75 million websites, WordPress security issues are also the most common. Sites running on popular standard CMS platforms are the most vulnerable. Any type of website is at risk; and if you are using a popular CMS like WordPress, Joomla or Umbraco, your site may be identified as a potential target for attack.

Most website security breaches don't involve stealing your data or changing a website's layout, but rather trying to use your server as an email relay for spam or setting up a temporary web server, often used to serve illegal files. Without a good firewall, hackers can scan your website and sensitive information like passwords, emails, or confidential files. Hackers can download and access malicious files to your system, overwrite existing files, block your website, and more.

MalCare reminds you that most hacks are due to vulnerabilities, so taking care of them will protect your site well enough from hackers and viruses. While MalCare cannot promise that this article will keep your website secure forever, we have given you some general security tips that will make it much harder for your website to be hacked. The security of your website plays a very important role in today's world, if your customers are not satisfied and trust your security system, they will not share their sensitive information with you.

Whether you're concerned about personal data, customer information, or the health of your online platform, you can follow a few simple steps to protect your website. Using strong passwords for the server and admin areas of your website is critical, but it's equally important to stick to strong passwords for your users to keep their accounts secure. Educate every CMS user about the importance of passwords and software updates.

Good website security starts with you - choose a reputable website builder or hosting provider, choose wisely how to manage your website, and go the extra mile to protect your passwords. To make the Internet more secure and develop content-rich and secure websites, web development companies can rely on a headless CMS approach that won't let you down with WordPress, Drupal, and other CMS platforms. Due to the size of WordPress, users mostly have to find and implement their own website security measures, a daunting task for many novice users. According to Sucuri, a provider of CMS security software, 94% of all infected websites in 2019 were on WordPress.

The process for changing the admin URL varies depending on the CMS you use. Changing the admin URL in Drupal is not as easy as in other CMS applications. To change the admin URL using Joomla!, you need to add an extension called JSecure to your CMS.

If the plugin is activated, go to Settings to change the admin URL. Scroll down the settings page and change the admin URL in this section, then click Save Changes to save the new URL. Go to the /wp-content/plugins folder and find the plugins folder that changes the login URL.

You can add a WordPress login link to the footer, sidebar, or pretty much any other widget-ready area in your theme. If you have multiple users on your WordPress site, it makes sense to add a WordPress login form to the sidebar or create a custom login page that matches the design and theme of your site. You can add a WordPress login link to your site's footer, sidebar, or menu.

After logging in, you will be redirected to your website's WordPress admin panel. If you are not already logged in and try to log in to the WordPress admin panel by adding /wp-admin, WordPress will automatically redirect you to the WordPress admin login page without any further action on your part. If your site URL is incorrect, you will not be able to log in because WordPress will try to redirect you to the wrong URL when you try to access the WordPress login page.

If you fix these errors, your WordPress site will start working and you will be able to login again. Another common reason why you can't login to wp-admin is because there is some kind of error on your site. If you have the wrong permissions on the wp-login.php file and the wp-admin folder, this may prevent you from logging into your WordPress dashboard. If you do not have the proper permission to access your website, when you try to access Sitefinity CMS, a message is displayed informing you of this.

The default URL for WordPress login is the same version of the URL you use to access your WordPress site, but with "/wp-admin" added to the end.

The login page is the gateway between your website and your site's dashboard, also known as the admin area. If you want to access the Joomla login or front end module, the URL is as follows. You must use this path if you need administrator access. In a typical WordPress installation with a good WordPress hosting provider, all you need to do is add /login/ or /admin/ to the end of your site's URL.

A common WordPress security tip is to change the URL of your login page, which you can easily do with various plugins. For example, if the WordPress security plugin has changed the login URL or the wp-admin folder has been moved. If your admin credentials are incorrect, your first step should be to use the built-in WordPress password recovery feature. If the password reset email doesn't work, you can manually change your password or create a new WordPress admin by editing your sites database using a tool called phpMyAdmin (which almost all WordPress hosts offer).

By changing your login URL, you can protect yourself from the obvious sign that your site is using a CMS by distancing yourself from any known issues. When you use the default URLs, you make yourself more vulnerable, a hacker will only need your username and password to enter the site. You can make yourself less of a target, better protect yourself from brute-force attacks, and reduce the bandwidth used by bots that repeatedly use the default login URL.

To be clear, not all URLs are bad, but a good rule of thumb is to only use short and easy-to-read URLs themselves, such as links to a website's home page. Re-enter your website URL in the address bar and add /admin at the end.

You must use lowercase letters to change or rename the admin URL path because admin URLs are case-sensitive. Now you need to change the status to "Yes" to use the custom admin url, after that you need to add the custom admin url. notes. After adding this to your wp-config.php file, you will no longer be able to change your site's URL from the WordPress dashboard - keep this in mind if you ever need to change your domain name in the future.

Fortunately, creating and activating an Overlay module is quick and easy. If you're running WordPress and using plugins, you can secure your CMS in just a few steps. You need to scroll down to the settings page to change the admin url and finally you need to click the button to update the new url. All CMSs provide another way to change the admin url and make it secure. First, you need to log into your WordPress dashboard with the correct username and password. If you're a new user, the "Welcome to WordPress" message will appear in the first place in your admin panel with helpful links to help you get started.

How to Protect Your Login Information

Creating a strong password is the first step a person can take to protect their devices and personal information. Password security involves using cybersecurity tools, best practices and procedures to create passwords that better protect personal information. Luckily, there are easy ways to make your passwords as secure as possible.

Consider using a password manager to store and secure your passwords, which can make longer, more complex passwords easier to use. In general, choose long and complex passwords, choose different ones for each service, and regularly change them to long ones... and if you want to memorize, use a password manager. All of the above methods help make your passwords more secure, but they are not very effective as the average person uses dozens of them.

By using different systems to generate passwords for various types of websites, such as social networking sites, financial institutions, and other membership sites, you can ensure that if a hacker compromises your algorithm, he cannot decrypt all the passwords at once. your account. To prevent damage, always use different passwords for different websites.

The change is bad, but the damage could be much greater if you reused your password for this site on other websites, so an attacker could also get into your accounts on those sites. When an attacker steals the password database for a site you use (such as LinkedIn or Yahoo), all you can do is change the password for that site.

If your password for one site is compromised, it can be used to log into your accounts on multiple sites. By choosing a unique password for each account, hackers who break into one account cannot use it to access all the others.

Many times, if one account is hacked, your data is no longer safe in other accounts that use the same login information, especially if you use the same password for multiple services. Not only can hackers use the same password to access your other important accounts, but you can also open the door to more people trying to break into many different websites.

Your password can access your private areas, so you might be thinking about the best way to create a strong password to protect your account from these cybercriminals. To keep your online accounts, information, and devices safe, you need to know how to create a strong password. To that end, online users must also use new and innovative ways to create strong passwords to keep their personal information safe.

It doesn't take much effort to make your devices, online identification and activities more secure. If you need to use the internet to access online banking while in a public place, there are a few things you can do to stay safe. This can prevent hackers from getting hold of your accounts and prevent your information (or money from online banking!) from being stolen!

While these actions may make it easier to remember passwords, they also make it easier for hackers to guess your passwords and access your banking information online. A password manager can help protect you from cybercriminals by creating and storing a unique, long and complex password for each of your online accounts. So-called app passwords help you stay safe when you log into a single app or service with your Yahoo account. Click "Account Security" to get to the main settings you need to know - you can enable the ubiquitous 2-step verification feature, as well as set up app passwords, which are one-time passwords that Yahoo generates for apps or specific services associated with your Yahoo account link.

Click "Advanced security settings" to view additional features and set up two-step verification, after which a trusted smartphone will become an additional requirement to sign in to your Microsoft account in addition to your username and password. This means that anyone who tries to log into your account on a new device will need a different code (sent via text message or an app on your phone) as well as your username and password. Often adding means linking your phone number to your account, so after entering your password you will be prompted for a security code sent directly to you. Using it ensures that if someone decrypts your account password, they can't log in unless they can log into your account unless they also get access to your code, which means they also have to own your mobile device.

Typically, brute force attacks are automated using lists of common usernames and passwords. Dictionary attacks are why we emphasize the use of various letters, numbers, and symbols when creating secure passwords.

Credential Stuffing Attacks Not to be confused with password spraying. Credential injection uses known passwords to access account information. Hackers can easily use passwords that have been previously stolen or otherwise exposed in automatic login attempts, called credential filling, to log into an account. One of the easiest ways for hackers to steal information is to get a set of username/password combinations from one source and try those same combinations elsewhere.

Before we get into editing, let's first look at the different ways to crack passwords so you understand the most common methods used today. Read on to find out how to create and manage better passwords, how to be notified when a breach occurs, and important tips to make your logins even more secure.

The key to your online security is strong passwords, but the challenge is creating different passwords that you can actually remember, or you risk developing a bad habit of using the same login credentials for multiple accounts. The following tips will come in handy if you frequently visit a lot of websites and are afraid of forgetting which password to use.

Part Three: Even If Your CMS Link is Protected, They Still Have Their Trump Cards

MySQL Injection

MySQL injection is an attack technique where an attacker can spoof a server to execute a malicious SQL command by injecting a malicious SQL command into a web form input field or a page request query string. SQL Injection is a web security vulnerability that allows attackers to view data they shouldn't be able to see, allowing an attacker to tamper with the queries an application makes against its database by injecting a malicious SQL injection payload. SQL injection is a code injection technique used to attack data-driven applications in which malicious SQL statements are entered into an input field to be executed (for example, SQL injection, also known as SQLI, is a common attack vector that exploits malicious SQL for internal database manipulation to access information that was not intended to be displayed.

When an application is vulnerable to SQLi, hackers can bypass the authentication process and manually inject SQL statements (or malicious payloads) into the database. Using SQL injection vulnerabilities, attackers can manipulate database data in the database (for example, get sensitive data in the database, arbitrarily change data in the database, delete the database, etc. A successful SQL injection vulnerability can read sensitive data from the database, modify Database data (i.e. insert, update or delete), perform administrative operations on the database, retrieve the contents of files present in the database management system, and in some cases even send commands to the operating system.

One of them demonstrates that SQL injection is not only an attack that targets web applications or web services, but can also be used to compromise server systems and steal data. SQL injection (SQLi) can affect any website or web application based on SQL database (MySQL, Oracle, Sybase, Microsoft SQL Server, Access, Ingres, etc.). The most common web application attack is SQL injection, which according to security reports such as the Verizon Data Breach Investigation Report, OWASP Lists, and others, is the result of a poorly coded application.

SQL injection is currently the most common form of web attack as web forms are very common, often miscoded, and hacking tools used to find and exploit weaknesses are widely available online. Web forms must allow database access for data entry and response, so SQL injection bypasses firewalls and endpoint security. Website features such as contact forms, login pages, support tickets, search functionality, feedback fields, shopping carts, and even functions that provide dynamic web page content are all susceptible to SQL injection attacks. , since the fields themselves submitted for visitor use SHOULD allow at least some SQL commands to be passed directly to the database.

SQL injection attacks allow attackers to falsify identities, tamper with existing data, cause failure issues such as transaction reversals or balance changes, ensure full disclosure of all data in a system, destroy data or otherwise make it inaccessible, and become database server administrators . SQL injection attacks are a class of injection attacks that use input from untrusted data sources to (dynamically) build and execute commands such as SQL, LDAP, shell, XML, and XPATH.

In this type of attack, the attack works on well-protected databases that don't return useful feedback or descriptive error messages. In this type of injection attack, the application displays the same response regardless of user input and database errors. In this type of attack, a Boolean query causes the application to provide different responses for valid or invalid results in the database.

The boolean based method sends SQL queries to the database to force the application to return a boolean result that is the result of TRUE or FALSE. Boolean - The attacker sends a SQL query to the database, asking the application for a result. This type of attack differs from others in that the hacker inserts additional queries into the original query, causing the database to receive more SQL queries.

This type of attack can be done by placing a UNION query in a vulnerable parameter that returns a dataset that is the union of the results of the first original query and the results of the second query. From there, the attacker writes a UNION SQL query for your search in order to take control of the generated SQL query and extract information it was not intended for. The attacker sends a prepared SQL query to retrieve, add, modify, or delete data from the database.

The attacker inserts arbitrary data (most commonly a database query) into a string that is ultimately executed by the database through the web application (e.g. the attacker initially attempts to use another injection method as an illegal/logically invalid query to Find the database type. Instead, the attacker creates an SQL statement that runs the database to create a connection to an external server under the attacker's control.

This type of injection attack is harder to use because it returns information when the SQL payload is provided to an application that returns a true or false response from the server. A practical example shows how an attacker can use a SQL Injection vulnerability to bypass application security and authenticate themselves as an administrator. A hack called SQL_MemCorrupt describes how to insert a record into a table that causes a corruption error in a SQL database and then query that table, which will crash the SQL database and core dump.

Error-based SQL injection vulnerabilities exist when error information generated by the database backend is returned to the end user, which can be used by the end user to proceed with other types of SQL injection attacks. If SQL injection is possible, a clever attacker can create user data to steal valuable data, bypass authentication, or corrupt database records.

In a nutshell, SQL injection, also known as SQLi, uses a website vulnerability as an input channel to target the database located at the back end of a web application, where the most sensitive and valuable information is stored. One of them suggests that SQL injection is not just an attack against web applications or web services, but can also be used to compromise server systems and steal data. It all depends on the capabilities of the attacker, but exploiting SQL injection vulnerabilities can even lead to a complete takeover of databases and web servers.

Due to the prevalence of a common database infrastructure, a SQL Injection error in one application can compromise other applications using the same database instance. An account server without administrator rights can also put an application at risk, especially if the database server is used by multiple applications and databases. In more serious cases, when the connection to the database server is made through an administrative account (for example, aroota in MySQL or asaa in MS SQL Server), an attacker can completely compromise the server's operating system.

In a serious case, such as a SQL injection bypass attack, attackers can gain unprecedented control over the entire system, as well as access and modify critical business or customer data. Attackers can access sensitive information, change web content and, in extreme cases, delete your data. So armed with literally nothing more than a web browser, some basic knowledge of SQL, and an internet connection, an attacker can exploit your web application's flaws: extract user data, detect or reset credentials, and use that as a point. for deeper attacks on your network.

The problem becomes especially acute, since the exploitation of the discovered vulnerabilities is not difficult and this is actively exploited (and abused) by cybercriminals on the Internet. In one case, attackers used a SQL injection vulnerability to create user accounts on a compromised server, enable remote desktop functionality, set up SMB shares and download malware, and destroy virtually everything stored in a database. As with almost all technological advances, new attack vectors have been discovered by hackers, and as long as relational databases have been used in web applications, SQL Injection attack vectors have also been used.

Some database programmers believe that stored procedures protect their code from SQL injection attacks. Stored procedures are just as vulnerable to injection attacks as any other SQL interaction when dealing with dynamically generated content. Stored procedures are also not immune to this vulnerability if dynamic SQL generation is used.

To avoid injection attacks, the SQL statements of applications connecting to the same database should be checked regularly. The third party or vendor must keep track of all application SQL statements connected to the database, including the documentation of all database accounts, prepared statements, and stored procedures. In addition, Imperva Database Security proactively monitors data access activity to identify any data access behavior that poses a risk or violates policy, whether from network SQL queries, compromised user accounts, or malicious insiders. .

In general, web frameworks prevent SQL injection attacks by providing simple methods for querying data so that developers aren't tricked into horribly vulnerable SQL string concatenation operators. The traditional approach to preventing SQL injection attacks is to treat them as an input validation problem and accept only characters from the security allow list or identify and avoid potentially dangerous disallow lists. Prevention techniques such as input validation, parameterized queries, stored procedures, and escape work well against a variety of attack vectors.

An attacker who wants to perform a SQL injection manipulates a standard SQL query to exploit unverified input vulnerabilities in a database. The attacker inserts arbitrary data, most commonly a database query, into a string that is eventually executed by the database through the web application (for example, this type of attack attempts to gather information about the type and structure of the web application's back-end database.

SQL injection forces an application to issue additional SQL commands to the database itself, usually to gain elevated access or cause the database to report more information than it should. Attackers can use SQL injection to steal or spoof data, compromise applications, and, in the worst case, gain administrative access to database servers. SQL injection is a code injection technique that allows hackers to inject malicious SQL statements into input fields for execution by the underlying SQL database.

A successful SQL injection attack can read sensitive data from a database, modify data (insert/modify/update/delete), execute administrative processes, and extract the contents of a specific file present on the database server, and can even run system-level operational commands . [3]. An attacker can use SQL commands in the input to modify the SQL statement that is executed by the database server. An attacker uses poorly filtered or incorrectly escaped characters embedded in SQL statements to parse variable data from user input.

Attackers take advantage of situations where developers often combine SQL statements with user-supplied parameters, and then insert SQL commands into those parameters to change the default SQL query. SQL and its variants can be complex, but attackers know very well how to create snippets of code that could compromise a database. If you haven't written anything in SQL before, it's easy to fall into the "oh, SQL is what you need to get data from a database" trap, and underestimating its power and complexity can lead directly to many of the security issues you'll encounter .When you insert the web application in front of the SQL database. There are tons of SQL queries going through your web application almost every time a page loads, whether it's a small toy site with tiny SQLite files, or a popular e-commerce site with millions of hits, it now requires a huge Database server cluster. Enterprise database. Supplier of your choice.

With the SQL query and SQL query results returned in the application response, an attacker can exploit the SQL injection vulnerability to extract data from other tables in the database. This means that the application will not return SQL query results or database error messages in its responses. In this type of injection attack, the application displays the same response regardless of user input and database errors.

Later, while processing another HTTP request, the application extracts the user input and embeds it in the SQL query in an insecure way. This type of attack differs from others in that the hacker inserts additional queries into the original query, causing the database to receive more SQL queries. This type of attack can be done by placing a UNION query in a vulnerable parameter that returns a dataset that is the union of the results of the first original query and the results of the second query.

In this type of attack, a Boolean query causes the application to provide different responses for valid or invalid results in the database. In this approach, the attacker devises a conditional statement, injects a vulnerable parameter, and delays gathering information based on database responses. The attacker first tries to find the database type using another injection method (such as an illegal/logically invalid query).

The attacker inserts arbitrary data, most commonly a database query, into a string that is eventually executed by the database through the web application (for example, the attacker uses a predefined time-based system function to control the database used by the Time- application). based - The attacker sends a SQL query to the database, which causes the database to wait (for a period in seconds) before it can respond.

Once the attacker determines which databases are being used on the back end, he attempts to execute various procedures using the injected code. The following example (Java) is INSECURE and allows an attacker to inject code into a query that will be executed by the database. An attacker can use SQL commands in the input to modify the SQL statement that is executed by the database server.

If the web application accepts this input without filtering it, an attacker can inject SQL statements through form fields and delete, copy, or modify the contents of the database. To bypass this security mechanism, SQL code must be entered in the input field. Controlled means that an attacker cannot modify the internal SQL query by injecting malicious input into the front end of the web page. The database server accepts user input and returns relevant values, indicating that an attacker can use malicious input to modify the internal query.

If your web page displays the results of a database query, an attacker can use the show table command, a command to view the tables in the database, and then selectively drop the tables if they wish. Even if an attacker throws an error in the SQL query, the response to the query may not be passed directly to the web page. The trick is not to make the query valid by entering the correct SQL commands.

When compiling HQL queries, you need to remember to inject and use the createQuery() function again, which works like a prepared statement. Execution is useful at every injection point, especially in internal SQL Server applications. Like SQL queries created in an application, stored procedures can also be maliciously injected. If creation cannot be avoided, the stored procedure must use appropriate input validation or escaping, as described in this article, to ensure that SQL code cannot be inserted into a dynamically generated query using any user input to the stored procedure.

If you then escape all user input using the appropriate escaping scheme for the database you are using, the DBMS will not confuse that input with developer-written SQL, avoiding any SQL injection vulnerabilities.

An attacker could use SQL injection to find other users' credentials in the database. Here, an attacker can log in as any user without a password by simply using a series of SQL comments to remove the password check from the query's WHERE clause. The above code can be used by commenting out part of the password and adding an always true condition.

This type of injection attack is more difficult to use because it returns information when the SQL payload is given to an application that returns a true or false response from the server. Direct SQL command injection is a technique in which an attacker creates or modifies existing SQL commands to reveal hidden data, ignore valuable data, or even execute dangerous system-wide commands on the database host. It does this by letting the application take user input and combine it with static parameters to create an SQL query.

Embedding a Backdoor To Your System

Backdoors are just some of the common ways hackers get into a network undetected to gain remote access to a computer. Backdoors allow hackers to gain control and control (C&C) of a target network undetected and can use legitimate websites or services to launch an attack. To get around the block, the hackers use a backdoor connection to connect the target system to the hackers' C&C server via outbound connections, as these are rarely blocked by firewalls.

To bypass this and deliver the second malware, attackers have been known to create a network connection utility or ping in the backdoor to bypass the service provider's security and intruder detection. An example of a simple backdoor is the following code snippet, which allows a hacker to execute a command on a website's server.

In practice, a backdoor can also be used by a developer as a legitimate way to access a website. Regardless of who creates the backdoor (developer or hacker), it is always a threat to the security of a website. Apple can explain in detail how Apple's technical implementation will maintain privacy and security in the proposed backdoor, but at the end of the day, even a well-documented, elaborate and narrowly targeted backdoor is still a backdoor.

A hacker who injects malicious code into a binary then repackages mobile apps and publishes them as a new (presumably legitimate) app disguised as a patch or crack, or surreptitiously (re)installs it on unsuspecting users' devices. You can directly access, view, modify and use unprotected binary code in mobile applications. Even non-malicious applications can make your mobile device vulnerable.

There are many types of malware that can affect your mobile device, from Trojans and backdoors to malicious code designed to steal valuable information such as online banking credentials. While iPhones can be hacked, more and more malware is targeting Android devices.

Mobile malware is nowhere near as popular as desktop malware, but these variants infect Google's Android operating system, iOS, and sometimes end up in official app repositories. Sometimes a mobile app can be hacked without any malware or hacking tools. It is possible to use a legitimate Android application such as a Trojan to exploit the user's real device.

The Trojan can use private APIs to install other Apple App Store software on the victim's device, thus bypassing any iOS security checks. Android phones can also fall prey to text messages with links to download malicious apps (the same scam is not common for iPhones, which are usually not jailbroken and thus cannot download apps from anywhere other than the App Store). A common method used by malware developers is to submit a mobile app that appears to be legitimate and then download malicious functions after the user base has been established, such as in the recent case of Google's Android OS app containing Google's Cerberus infiltration. Play Trojan.

In addition, there are commercial spy apps that require physical access to be downloaded to the phone—often by people well known to the victim, such as a partner or parent—and that can track everything that happens on the device. Often, third-party antivirus apps provide little extra functionality as they are much more limited in what they can do than what your mobile OS's built-in security features already do. There are some third-party tools and scripts on the web that promise more reliable results in the backdoor of even more new Android apps on the web.

We hope that knowing the backdoors of the most common existing applications will help you make better decisions about which applications to install and which software to test for vulnerabilities. We recommend that you download and install an antivirus software solution for your mobile device, however, you will probably be completely safe as long as you do not jailbreak your phone and only download .APK apps from trusted sources and not third parties. repositories. Let's move your malicious app to our web server so we can deliver it quickly to our target android device.

When the malicious app launches, it starts the standard WhatsApp installation process, but runs a backdoor in the background and sends a reverse shell connection to the attacker. GhostCtrls base64 decodes and writes strings from resource files at runtime, which is actually a malicious APK. The main APK has a backdoor feature commonly known as com.android.engine to mislead users into thinking it is a legitimate system app.

Using information gathered through code analysis tools and activities, mobile application binaries can be reverse engineered and valuable code (including source code), sensitive data or proprietary intellectual property can be extracted from the application and reused or repackage. According to

McAfee's 2020 Mobile Threats Report, more than half of mobile malware "lurks" on devices without a home screen icon, hijacking devices to display unwanted ads, post fake reviews, or steal information for sale. Or used to hold victims hostage.

We can get an idea of who our victim is by activating the front or back camera of our stock Android phone. This command will give us the device's GPS coordinates, which we can simply find on Google Maps.

A backdoor in an access system can take the form of an encrypted user/password combination that allows access to the system. The application's backdoor access can be encrypted to provide a cybercriminal with remote access to a compromised system. In a backdoor attack, malicious code can take control of an application to extract trade secrets from corporate databases, steal employee information to steal identities, delete important files, and spread from server to server.

Once inside, cybercriminals can use backdoors to steal personal and financial data, install other malware, and hijack devices. Hackers can even remotely access your device from their computer through a backdoor, accessing all your files and software from the comfort of your home.

By using a backdoor to gain superuser access to your system, cybercriminals can take control of your computer remotely, registering it in a network of hacked computers (also known as a botnet). Once your device is compromised, backdoors can be used to spread malware to your device (such as cryptojackers, rootkits, or ransomware), steal your data and track your activities, or simply install malware that crashes your device Virus. Hackers can use malware to install backdoors on your device, exploit vulnerabilities in your software, or even install backdoors directly into your device's hardware/firmware. A hacker can only place a backdoor on your site if they have direct access to the site.

To remove a backdoor, you need to find the specific branch of code that gives hackers unauthorized access to your site, and then completely remove that code. Also, the backdoor code can be hidden in many different areas of your site's code. Hackers can scrutinize your code looking for security vulnerabilities that allow them to take control of your website using any platform or script vulnerability. Hackers find a way to inject malicious JavaScript code into your pages, which can then infect the devices of all website visitors exposed to the code.

Many types of malicious code can harm your computer by finding entry points that lead to your valuable data. Malicious code can cause backdoors, security breaches, information and data theft, and other potential damage to files and computer systems. Business systems that frequently use reusable components can be particularly vulnerable to malicious code, as a single code flaw or bug that opens the door to attackers can become a weakness that spreads across multiple applications, causing a serious security issue. Mistakes made by developers when designing and writing mobile application code lead to security holes and can be exploited by attackers.

To protect your mobile device, you may need different security measures than to protect your computer. Mobile application protection is similar to desktop application protection; however, this is often more difficult as mobile applications often rely on external connectivity to internal back-end systems, which increases the potential attack surface.

By making security by design a challenge in application development, you can create useful, fun, and secure applications. If you built your website with a content management system (CMS), you can enhance your website with security plugins that proactively prevent website hacking. When it comes to WordPress security, you can do a lot. Block your website. Prevent hacks and exploits from affecting your e-commerce website or blog. Unfortunately, many WordPress site owners cannot enforce 2-step verification, and hackers can easily compromise up to 30,000 sites in a day using a brute force attack.

Hackers may want to steal, change, or delete information on your device, and often do so by installing malware (software used for malicious purposes) that you may not even know exists. In the world of cybersecurity, a backdoor is any method by which authorized and unauthorized users can bypass normal security measures and gain advanced user access (also known as root access) to a system, computer, network, or software application. In addition to exposing sensitive data such as private company information, backdoors can also allow attackers to become advanced persistent threats (APTs). From there, backdoors can be used to access privileged information, such as passwords, corrupt or delete data on hard drives, or transmit information over automated fabric networks.

An asymmetric backdoor can only be exploited by the attacker hosting it, even if the full implementation of the backdoor is publicly available (eg, by publishing, by reverse engineering discovery and disclosure, etc.). We know that backdoors are like secret entrances to your computer. The aptly named "backdoor" vulnerability exposes hackers to covert steps by bypassing secure encryption to access WordPress sites using unusual methods: wp-Admin, SFTP, FTP, etc.

Software developers create these backdoor accounts so they can quickly log in and out of applications as they are written, test their applications, and fix software bugs (i.e. since many of these tools are open source, their code readily available). - both to well-meaning developers and malicious hackers. With the help of debugging tools, software developers can find problems with the code and hackers can use them to break the code.

Software developers and legitimate hackers use debugging tools to check code line by line. Hackers can run debugging protections to detect when a debugging tool is being used to detect changes they are making to code. IT security professionals can use debugging protections to detect when a hacker is running a debugging program as part of an attack. Here, the application will inject debug detection code into various parts of the application and use the result to change the normal behavior of the application so that, for example, it does not communicate properly with the server, does not save data, etc.

Open Source Vulnerability

Open source code is vulnerable precisely because of its openness, because all users can see the same code, including attackers. While the vulnerability still exists, attackers can write and inject code to exploit it. Hackers using it can easily break into internal systems because they don't have to crack the password to abuse the latest password.

It scans for vulnerabilities, but also allows you to exploit discovered vulnerabilities, such as operating system command injection, SQL injection, path traversal, and more. It acts as a countermeasure against threats exploiting known and unknown vulnerabilities by implementing a layer of security policies and rules to block the path of successful exploits in and out of vulnerabilities. Use is risky and exposes some insurmountable vulnerabilities. This cybersecurity breach could be as simple as creating a link and convincing users to click it, or it could be something more sinister.

Software often has security holes that hackers can exploit to cause damage. Many threats use legitimate open source penetration testing and system administration tools to successfully exploit vulnerabilities.

There are many tools for exploiting web applications; however, those mentioned above cover some of the main areas where web applications are most vulnerable to security vulnerabilities. Below are some of the tools used by hackers to exploit vulnerabilities.

An exploit is a means by which hackers use a vulnerability to carry out an attack. A threat is a real or hypothetical event in which one or more exploits use a vulnerability to carry out an attack. A security vulnerability is a flaw in the code or misconfiguration of a system through which attackers can directly gain unauthorized access to a system or network.

Once hackers have discovered vulnerabilities in systems and platforms, systems and platforms, they can start looking for ways to exploit those vulnerabilities. This is known as exploitation of a vulnerability and allows hackers to exploit systems and platforms. Sometimes hackers or attackers notice a vulnerability before software developers.

Security First Check Point says 37% of UK corporate networks have been exploited, with hackers scanning the internet for possible targets. Chinese tech giant Alibaba reported to the Apache Software Foundation on Nov. 24 a vulnerability found in the Apache open-source software used to run websites and other web services. Chinese hackers are already exploiting a well-armed software flaw that wreaks havoc online, and experts have warned it is the worst threat they have faced in decades. A recently discovered vulnerability in a widely used software repository is wreaking havoc on the Internet, forcing cyber defenders to work while hackers struggle to exploit the flaw.

U.S. government warned the private sector about the Log4j vulnerability and looming risks. Dubbed Log4j, the vulnerability is related to a software library widely used by software developers. In one of the largest cybersecurity incidents in recent memory, Log4j exploited a vulnerability in a key open source logging tool used by millions of applications around the world.

Of the approximately 60 application security vulnerabilities reported by the open community, OWASP's top 10 vulnerabilities include the vulnerabilities that are most commonly exploited. It focuses on the top 10 web vulnerabilities identified by the Open Web Application Security Project (OWASP), an international non-profit organization dedicated to improving software security around the world. Cybersecurity researchers on Tuesday identified nine security flaws affecting three open source projects—EspoCRM, Pimcore and Akaunting—that are widely exploited by multiple small and medium-sized businesses and, if successfully exploited, could open the way for more sophisticated EspoCRM attacks. . Therefore, it is very important that the operating system is kept secure, otherwise the operating system is at risk of being exploited by hackers.

DOM Based Cross Site Scripting

Why traditional XSS recovery methods are ineffective against DOM-based XSS, and what you can do to prevent your web application from being vulnerable to such cross-site scripting vulnerabilities. Cross-site scripting, also known as XSS, is a client-side attack that executes code in the victim's browser by injecting JavaScript into a web application and navigating the victim to a vulnerable URL. Cross-site scripting attacks are caused by XSS vulnerabilities caused by inherent security vulnerabilities in client-side scripting languages such as JavaScript and HTML. Like all other cross-site scripting (XSS) vulnerabilities, this type of attack relies on insecure processing of user input in HTML pages.

In short, cross-site scripting (XSS) allows an attacker to "hijack" HTML pages, trick users and steal sensitive data by redirecting links and rewriting web page content. XSS is a type of injection where a malicious script is injected into secure and trustworthy websites. XSS works by exploiting a vulnerability in a website that causes malicious JavaScript code to be returned when users visit it.

By injecting malicious client-side script into a trusted website, cross-site XSS script tricks an application into sending malicious code through a browser that it believes is from a trusted source. While traditional XSS uses vulnerable server-side CGI scripts to directly generate code in served pages, DOM-based XSS uses vulnerable JavaScript scripts that run directly in users' browsers.

The key difference between other XSS attacks and DOM-based attacks is that in other XSS attacks, the malicious script is executed when the vulnerable web page is initially loaded, while the DOM-based attack is performed after the page is loaded. In DOM-based cross-site scripting, the HTML source code and the attack response will be exactly the same, i.e. the vulnerability payload cannot be found in the response. After executing such malicious code on a page, attackers could use this DOM-based cross-site scripting vulnerability to steal cookies from users' browsers or modify the behavior of a web application page with malicious intent. This type of attack is carried out using JavaScript in users' browsers.

An attack like this type of attack is guaranteed to bypass any server-side filtering attempt to protect users. Server-side attack detection tools will not be able to detect the attack. Because there are cases where the payload never reaches the server, preventing this vulnerability is not a server-side task. Any client code that refers to document.location, for example, can be vulnerable to a fragment attack, in which case the payload is never sent to the server.

For example, if client-site JavaScript modifies the DOM tree of a web page based on input fields or GET parameters, without validating the input, malicious code may be executed. A DOM-based XSS attack can be successfully performed even if the server does not inject any malicious code into the web page by exploiting a vulnerability in JavaScript running in the web browser. ``type-0 XSS") is an XSS attack in which the payload is executed by altering the DOM "environment" in the victim's browser used by the original client-side script in order to execute client-side code "out of Unexpected " way.

Attackers typically exploit stored XSS payloads by injecting XSS payloads into popular pages of a website, or by passing a link to victims to trick them into viewing pages that contain stored XSS payloads, stored XSS payloads. What makes a cross-site scripting attack even worse is that the victim, neither the user nor the affected application, is often unaware that the victim is being attacked. Attackers can run JavaScript of their choice on the victim's machine, so XSS can be used to execute various security threats and/or combined with other web vulnerabilities to exploit serious security vulnerabilities. To gain access, XSS attacks typically use social engineering techniques or launch phishing attacks to send victims to malicious websites.

Obviously, in situations where the payload can be completely hidden, online detection (IDS) and online prevention products (IPS, Web Application Firewall) cannot fully protect against this exploit, assuming that a vulnerable script can actually be run. from a known position. This assumes that an attacker has already discovered an archived cross-site scripting vulnerability in the target web application and can trick or guarantee that the victim will visit the page containing the archived payload. A prerequisite is that the vulnerable site has an HTML page that insecurely uses data from document.location, document.URL, or document.referrer (or any other object that an attacker can influence). In addition to the general measures described on the DOM Vulnerabilities page, you should avoid dynamically writing data from any untrusted source into an HTML document.

YOUR SYSTEM'S SWEETSPOTS: CEO'S ADVICE ON BASIC CYBER SECURITY

Now, no matter how complex your web application is, the only thing that can lead to an XSS DOM vulnerability is code in one of your policies, and you can block it even further by restricting policy creation. In fact, even other types of web protection such as web application firewalls or generic protections such as ASP.NET request validation will not protect you from DOM-based XSS attacks. Developers and maintainers (and reviewers) of a site should be familiar with DOM-based XSS vulnerability detection methods, as well as methods to protect against them, which differ from those applicable to standard XSS.

Cross-site scripting (XSS) describes a web security vulnerability that allows attackers to disrupt user activity by injecting malicious scripts designed to hijack vulnerable applications. In the stored XSS example, a malicious script may have been sent through an input field to a web server that did not perform adequate validation and permanently stored the script in a database. The script code either incorrectly validates the input or does not encode the correct output, providing an opportunity for an attacker to inject malicious script to launch an XSS attack.

DOM-based XSS, also known as XSS Type-0, is an XSS attack in which the attack payload is executed by modifying the DOM in the victim's browser. DOM-based XSS vulnerabilities differ in that the attack occurs entirely within the browser, specifically the DOM (Document Object Model) of the current web page. In DOM-based XSS, the HTML source code and attack response remain unchanged, so malicious input is not included in the server response. Traditional Reflex XSS aims to embed client-side data into server-side code in HTML documents, while in DOM-based XSS, malicious payloads are referenced and executed in the client-side (browser) environment.

DOM-based XSS is a cross-site scripting vulnerability that allows attackers to inject a malicious payload into a web page by manipulating the client's browser environment. Cross-site scripting (XSS) is a security vulnerability that allows attackers to execute malicious code in a victim's web browser, bypassing the same-origin policy. Cross-site scripting, also known as XSS, is a client-side attack in which code is executed in the victim's browser by injecting JavaScript into a web application and navigating the victim to a vulnerable URL. Archival cross-site scripting is very dangerous because the payload is not visible to any client-side XSS filters, and an attack can affect multiple users without further attacker intervention.

By definition of an XSS client, any vulnerability or attack that does not use a web server to deliver a payload to the victim is an XSS client. An XSS client occurs when the DOM is updated through an insecure JavaScript call with data provided by an untrusted user. While DOM-based XSS occurs when data from an untrusted source is processed by writing data to a potentially dangerous sink in the DOM, reflected XSS occurs when an application receives data in an HTTP request and returns it in an unsafe manner. way to include such data in an immediate response. Reflected XSS occurs when a web application immediately returns user input in an error message, search result, or any other response that includes some or all of the user input as part of the request, but does not display the data securely in the browser, and There is no need to permanently store user-provided data.

XSS attacks based on server-side embedding of user data are classified as "non-persistent" (or "reflected") and "persistent" (or "archival"). DOM-based attacks go largely undetected if the attacker avoids server-side authentication methods, while traditional reflected XSS attacks are easily detected using intrusion detection systems and logs. DOM-based XSS vulnerabilities typically occur when JavaScript takes data from an attacker-controlled source, such as a URL, and passes it to a dynamically executable receiver, such as eval() or innerHTML.

Developers and maintainers (and reviewers) of a site should be familiar with DOM-based XSS vulnerability detection methods, as well as methods to protect against them, which differ from those applicable to standard XSS. Let's dig a little deeper to understand the possible sources or entry points that attackers can use to perform XSS DOM attacks, as well as ``sinks" or DOM objects where they can execute malicious code. An attacker can run JavaScript of their choice on the victim's machine, so XSS can be used to execute various security threats and/or used in conjunction with other web vulnerabilities to exploit a serious security vulnerability.

While the results of a successful attack may be similar, the three types of XSS differ significantly in how malicious JavaScript payloads are injected into users' browsers. While this seems almost counter-defining or common sense, there are actually two well documented examples of XSS attacks described above. This type of attack is usually combined with phishing as a delivery mechanism to force the user to click on a link and run the JavaScript it contains.

Once the malicious JavaScript is injected, the attacker waits for the malicious JavaScript to run or sends it to an unsuspecting end user. The payload of the attackers is exposed in the client-side script at run time. It is important to remember that when using a DOM based DOM, it is not processed by the web server, the victim just needs to click on the payload ready link and the payload rendering is handled on the client side.

DOM-based XSS allows attackers to manipulate DOM objects that appear on a page, usually using a payload created in a URL. A third type of XSS, as defined by Amit Klein [1] who published the first article on the issue, is a form of XSS in which the entire flow of infected data from source to destination occurs in the browser, i.e. data The source is in the DOM, the destination is in the DOM, and the data flow never leaves the browser. Mutant XSS makes it extremely difficult to detect or clean up in a website's application logic. It's similar to Reflected XSS, but the difference is that when the DOM changes, the data may never reach the server (which changes how it's delivered). / should be relaxed because server-side filters can be inefficient).

This makes DOM-based XSS attacks more difficult for web application firewalls (WAFs) and security engineers parsing server logs for detection, since they will never see the attack. When the victim opens the vulnerable web page in the browser, the XSS payload is sent to the victim's browser as part of the HTML code (just like a legitimate comment). If the victim has administrative privileges on the target application, a successful XSS attack can be used to escalate privileges and then execute code on the server (read our analysis of the Jira incident on apache.org to see how this happened) .

Part Four: Passwords, Login Names ...... Piece of Cake!

Usual Tricks for Hackers to Crack Your Password

In this part, I will share with you the some most common methods that hackers use to get your password. To help you understand how hackers get your passwords, whether they're secure or not, we've compiled a list of ten top password cracking methods used by hackers.

Today, you can even find specialized password cracking tools that cannot be used solely for illegal purposes. Phishing is probably the most common method hackers use to get your passwords because of the cost and ease of creation.

This is by far one of the best ways to protect your accounts from hackers - even if they know your password, they won't be able to access your account. This is the easiest way to prevent hackers from guessing your credentials, but the password can still be stolen and used by an attacker using various methods such as keyloggers or MiTM attacks.

The longer a password stays the same, the more likely hackers will find a way to crack it. If you can read the password as a word or phrase, hackers using automated tools will be able to guess it.

An interesting way to create a strong and secure password is to use the first letter or number of a sentence. While they are easier to remember, for added security, it is recommended that you use a completely random passphrase to prevent a hacker from guessing your password using your personal information.

The best passwords don't have obvious combinations of numbers or letters. That means easy-to-remember passwords with names, words, and dates won't help. Also, using two common dictionary words does not make the password any more secure against attacks.

A dictionary attack exploits the fact that many people will use catchy phrases as passwords, which are usually whole words glued together. Hackers can use many tricks, dictionary attacks if you use lowercase and uppercase letters, combinations of many letters in characters with international characters such as a vowel with an umlaut, which will eliminate any password hacker. Hackers repeatedly use dictionary programs and try different combinations of words to crack your password.

The hackers crack using the Rainbow table, a pre-computed hash list of possible password combinations. In the simplest way, you can reduce the rainbow table to a list of pre-computed hashes - the numeric values used to encrypt the password.

The rainbow tables we're talking about are used to crack passwords and are just another tool in the ever-growing arsenal of hackers. Using Rainbow Tables allows you to crack passwords in a very short time compared to brute force methods, however the tradeoff is that Rainbow Tables require a lot of space (sometimes terabytes) to store. and cheap these days, so it doesn't really matter to hackers.

Attacks on Rainbow tables can be prevented using a number of methods, including the salt method, which involves adding random data to the password before hashing. You can also get precomputed rainbow tables to crack vulnerable operating systems (e.g. Windows XP, Vista, Windows 7) and applications that use MD5 and SHA1 as password hashing mechanisms (still used by many web application developers hashing algorithm) on the password.). To get around this, hackers maintain and share directories that record proper passwords and hashes, often created from previous hackers, reducing the time it takes to break into a system (for brute force attacks).

Cracking passwords using password jetting depends on the hacker's computing power and the platform they're trying to crack, as most platforms lock out an account after a few failed attempts. In password spraying, hackers use a list of common passwords to automatically try to log in.

Unfortunately, it's this ease of use that means that passwords are still the primary method of authenticating users, so it's important that we all be aware of the various methods used by hackers to gain access to this secret code. Hackers know that many passwords are poorly designed, so password attacks will continue to be an attack method as long as passwords are in use. If you want to keep your accounts secure, you need to use a really random, long, and complex password, and use completely different passwords for each account.

However, as important as passwords, about 52% still use the same password for multiple accounts, and 24% use regular password options that are easy to crack. If a hacker gains access to one of the passwords, he can easily guess all your other sites by replacing "fac" with letters that might match other sites (or by finding out what algorithm you have).

It is very likely that one or two passwords will fall through the cracks and fall directly into the hacker network. On average, it takes about two seconds for a hacker to crack an 11-character password that only uses numbers. If you consider a password to be made up of letters, numbers and symbols that are about 100 combinations per character, a five digit password would be 10 billion combinations, which seems like a long time, but a hacker can crack such a password in 10 seconds.

It may then take as long as it takes for the password cracker to attempt to crack the code without notifying the target system or individual user. Hackers collect compromised usernames and passwords into a list of targets to attack other networks and systems using a technique called credential reuse. A password attack is simply an attempt by a hacker to steal your password.

Password crackers are more likely to look at this information and make some assumptions, usually correct ones, when trying to crack consumer-grade passwords without resorting to dictionary or brute force attacks. guess. Even with all the modern programs and algorithms that exist today, sometimes the most efficient way to obtain passwords is to use common logic or password themes.

The Dark Web (Where Breached Data are sold)

The dark web is a dangerous place where hackers can buy and sell your personal information like social security numbers, medical records and credit card numbers to the highest bidder. This means that hackers can easily steal your personal data and use it to carry out more dangerous attacks or sell it on the dark web for thousands of dollars.

Criminals can share or sell leaked data on the dark web without taking any action, allowing companies to find stolen material before criminals use it. Criminals, however, also deal with things like malware, stolen data, and stolen personal data. Criminals may sell goods such as illegal drugs, child pornography, or stolen confidential information.

While the dark web is often used for legitimate activities, cybercriminals can form communities, hire hackers and sell illegally obtained data. The anonymity provided by the dark web is often exploited by hackers and criminals who trade illicit goods, services, and stolen personal data.

Because the Dark Web is difficult and dangerous to navigate, and many public websites are not indexed by search engines, data protection technologies are needed to protect data that could be compromised by a cyberattack. By taking a proactive stance on data protection and not burying your head in the sands of the Dark Web, you can stay one step ahead of cybercriminals. Don't be left in the dark when it comes to data breaches and corporate security vulnerabilities.

If your information has been compromised, we can help you take steps to correct and restore security and peace of mind. Contact one of our Managed IT Specialists today for a complete network assessment and Dark Web scanning, and how we can help you support your IT team with personalized IT support and simplify your business security. While most of the stolen sensitive information comes from large-scale data breaches that have affected countless companies over the years, there are a few simple steps you can take to protect yourself.

Identity thieves often buy and sell personal information on the dark web after a data breach or hack, wanting to profit from your good name and any numbers or information about you. Hackers responsible for corporate data breaches often post stolen information on the "dark web" for others to buy and use for profit. It's no news that the dark web is flooded with stolen data products, from stolen credit card information and hacked payment service accounts to hacked social media accounts.

Criminals are selling your stolen personal data on the "dark web" for as little as $1, mostly through your fault, according to a new report released Wednesday. Hacked personal data may seem more secure than other malicious material sold on the dark web, but according to Emily Wilson, vice president of research at cybersecurity firm Terbium Labs, the cybersecurity firm Terbium Labs is in the hands of criminals. Serious and potentially dangerous consequences. Darknet criminals can determine how and when to pretend to be a persuasive reporter or event participant if the security of your data is compromised.

Once your personal data is up for sale, buyers can use it for financial gain or for doxing, a practice in which attackers publicly disclose personal information about you to the public. Unfortunately, once your leaked personal information is made public, it cannot be removed, stopped being sold, or prevented from being used by those who buy it. It is much easier and less stressful to prevent your data from being stolen.

You can minimize data leakage to the dark side by rethinking who should have access to customer and company data and when. For example, when you run a free check with the Auras Identity Guard Dark Web Scanner, we specifically evaluate the risk of identity theft, account theft, title and credit theft, spam and automated calls, and the likelihood that brokers' data could sell your personal information. data. Information.

Using the Tor browser, Internet users can access the Dark Web to communicate and share securely without the risk of it being traced back to their real identity. This allows users to connect to the deep web without fear that their activities will be tracked or their browser history exposed.

The underground ecosystem is the part of cyberspace considered vital to the criminal community, where criminals can acquire and sell tools, services, and data for a variety of illicit activities. Secretive hackers are known to monetize any data they can steal or buy and keep adding services so that other scammers can successfully commit scams both online and in person," says a report published by Dell SecureWorks. Businesses of all sizes All face significant risk. Company data leaks when employee accounts are hacked; once criminals get in, they can use the stolen data for various fraudulent schemes, such as business email compromises, fraudulent invoicing, and labor fraud. Worse Yes, research shows that most companies either do not protect their sensitive data or use traditional methods of security, which are largely ineffective, leaving them vulnerable to cyberattacks.

A seemingly endless stream of hacks and data breaches has included video games Fortnite, Dunkin Donuts and Dow Jones & Company. Tiny personal data — names, email addresses, phone numbers, social security numbers, and postal addresses — leaked in every major data breach piles up in a dark corner of the internet, the dark web. According to RSA, a consumer account can cost as little as $1 on the dark web — meaning anyone can buy at least one stolen account; it also means hackers need to acquire a lot of data to use it, which can be very important to you Both good and bad.

Part Five: The Solutions

How to Prevent MySQL Injection and Backdoor Injection with Better Coding Practice

i) How To Use The Mysqli_Real_Escape String Function To Prevent Mysql Injection

mysqli_real_escape_string($conn depends on the type of database and the php library you are using, see the php library documentation for more information on escaping user input. If you are using a MySQL server and the MySQLi library to access your database, mysqli_real_escape_string($ conn , $string) will accept two parameters, a MySQLi connection and a $string, and successfully escape user input to prevent SQL injection attacks. database Note that once we run the query through the mysqli_real_escape_string function, it is clean, clean and safe to use with MySQL.

One last thing to consider when using mysql_real_escape_string to clear data; mysql_real_escape_string() does not escape SQL wildcards for the LIKE operator. The important thing to remember here is that you must always quote the escaped parameter when using mysql_real_escape_string(), otherwise a SQL injection vulnerability will be created. To escape Catherine Oliri's string value, you can use PHP's str_replace function to replace a single quote with a sequence of backslashes and quotes, but it's best to use mysql_real_escape_string to do this for you. Escaping is just a way to tell MySQL that it's not a single quote that ends a string, but part of the string itself, and should be treated as such.

Mysql_real_escape_string() has been adopted by many to escape single quotes in strings while preventing SQL injection attacks. As mentioned earlier in this article, the mysql_real_escape_string parameter must be quoted to avoid SQL injection (regardless of the data type). When writing an application, any string that can contain these special characters must be escaped successfully before the string can be used as a data value in an SQL statement sent to SQL Server. A popular, albeit error-prone, and ultimately doomed way to prevent injection is to try to escape any character in SQL that has a special meaning.

If you use prepare() and bind_param() as an alternative to inserting arbitrary string values into SQL statements, you can avoid all character escaping issues (on the PHP side). You can see some code that uses various other PHP functions to handle escaping; this is usually a bug as well. Use escape sequences in SQL statements to tell the driver that the escaped portion of the SQL string should be treated differently. Escape or unescape SQL strings to remove traces of offending characters that might interfere with execution.

It is absolutely not applicable to SQL and cannot secure your query even if it is used as a string escaping function. Returns a string with a backslash in front of characters that need to be escaped in database queries, etc. The addlashes function takes a string as an argument and returns a string with all the problematic characters as an automatically escaped single quote. The addlashes function (string $str) works for escaping characters and is mainly used for database queries that don't have escaping functionality in PHP.

This function should always be used (with some exceptions) to ensure data security before sending a query to MySQL. This ensures that the statement and values are not parsed by PHP before they are sent to the database server (preventing a possible attacker from injecting malicious SQL). Any parameters sent using a prepared statement will simply be treated as strings (although the database engine may perform some optimizations, so of course the parameters can also be numbers). You can create SQL statements with well-formatted pieces of data, but if you don't fully understand the details, you should always use prepared statements and parameterized queries.

In a typical PHP application that formats an SQL string separately (partly in the query and partly elsewhere), it's very likely that some parts of the formatting could simply be omitted. Looking at the sequence of these examples, it would seem that creating SQL with named placeholders might seem like an edge when you can concatenate the SQL into a string and be done with it. Using in the first place means that your variables are not query strings that would accept arbitrary SQL input, however some parameters of certain types are definitely needed.

This function is used to create a valid SQL string that can be used in an SQL statement. Whereas `` escaping '' should only denote a certain part of the string's formatting. The `` '' character in a string enclosed in `` `` quotes requires no special handling and should not be duplicated or escaped.

When using parentheses to escape a single character, the escaped character becomes a separate token in the query. MySQL recognizes the escape sequences, "Special Character Escape Sequences", "Special Character Escape Sequences". As mentioned earlier, automatic value escaping on the server is sometimes considered a security feature against SQL injection.

The same degree of security can be achieved with raw statements if input values are stored correctly, so this demonstrates that validating data as intval() is a good idea for integer values before sending any requests, moreover, preventing malicious user data before sending request is an honest and efficient approach. Prevention techniques such as input validation, parameterized queries, stored procedures, and escape work well against a variety of attack vectors. In order to work around to correctly execute queries and prevent SQLi (SQL Injection)/Storage and/or XSS Reflection, it is recommended to follow the basics first and then ensure that nothing is included that can be exploited for SQLi or XSS. archiving/mirroring or, even worse, remote downloading of images and scripts. Note that this does not prevent SQL injection when double-quoted literals are used, it just makes it less likely (because normal, harmless queries will fail).

ii) How To Use Php Data Objects (Pdo) To Safely Execute The Sql Statements To Prevent MySQL Injection

When preparing an SQL statement, the database processes the SQL and prepares it for execution, but does not actually execute any code in the database. Parameterized queries are a means of precompiling an SQL statement so that you can then specify parameters for executing the statement. When processing SQL queries that contain user input, use prepared statements, also known as parameter queries. If you properly parameterize SQL queries, all user input passed to the database is treated as data and cannot be confused with part of a command.

If an attacker enters an SQL command, the parameter query will treat it as untrusted input and the database will not execute the injected SQL command. Direct SQL command input is performed by the application through user input and combined with static parameters to create an SQL query. Include allows an attacker to inject SQL into a query, causing the following code to send an invalid query to the MySQL database.

This type of attack is based on sending an SQL query that causes the application to return different results depending on whether a certain condition included in the query is true or false. Due to incorrect data validation, an attacker can issue a valid SQL statement that changes the logic of the original query used by the application to the original query used by the application. As we can see in the include/search.php code (lines 25-45), the SQL query is generated without any input being properly escaped.

The query returns a non-empty dataset for any potential logins using the entire "users" table database. The $sql value will be the string ``SELECT * FROM user WHERE id=8" and the query will succeed. All you need to do is pass parameters to the database query itself using the Parameters.Add() call as shown here.

This function associates parameters with an SQL query and tells the database what those parameters are. We're trying to get away from the SQL query field parameter where the application used the input to become something else. We form the form, add another field, and write the SQL in the name attribute.

Using the insert interface, we can inject SQL and display any error messages received. We can take advantage of the same interface by retrieving data from other existing tables in the database using the UNION SQL command. In order to use delete, insert, select or update methods later, we need to create a table in the database. Obviously, you can create a table by executing an SQL statement, so we use the run method for that.

In the code above, we store the SQL statement in the $sql variable and then use the run method to execute the statement. The stored procedure is still vulnerable to the SQL Injection attack because we construct the SQL query to be executed as a string by concatenating multiple strings instead of using auto-binding support. The difference between stored procedures is that the SQL code for the stored procedure is stored in the database itself and called by the application, while prepared statements are "prepared" whenever they need to be executed.

A prepared SQL statement works very similarly, instead of assembling the query string directly and executing it, it stores the prepared statement, populates it with data, and collects and cleans it for you at runtime. Prepared statements require more lines of PHP code than calling the old mysqli_query, but they are safer and repeated calls can be faster. Parameter queries force you to define an SQL query and use placeholders for user-supplied variables in the query. An attacker can use SQL injection (SQLi) to create a web application process and execute the injected SQL statement as part of an existing SQL query.

Direct SQL command injection is a technique where an attacker creates or modifies existing SQL commands to reveal hidden data or ignore valuable data, or even execute dangerous system-level commands on a database host. For example, use mysql_real_escape_string() in PHP to escape characters that might result in an unintended SQL command. If you are using an older version of PHP (5.5 or lower, which is common in shared hosting), it is recommended that all user input be handled through a function called mysql_real_escape_string(). Another thing a PHP user might think of is the familiar escape function that "makes your data safe" as falsely claimed in the PHP manual for centuries.

Unfortunately, the usual escape function will only help if the injection code contains quotes or other characters that this function works with. If you then escape all user input using the appropriate escaping scheme for the database you are using, the DBMS will not confuse that input with developer-written SQL, avoiding any SQL injection vulnerabilities. If creation cannot be avoided, the stored procedure must use appropriate input validation or escaping, to ensure that any user-entered data for the stored procedure cannot be used to insert SQL code into a dynamically generated query.

The helper function above will take the SQL code and insert it into the query. This ensures that the statement and values are not parsed by PHP before they are sent to the database server (preventing a possible attacker from injecting malicious SQL). If no SQL errors occurred, the insert method will return the number of new rows created.

If MySQL/ Backdoors are Injected Into Your Systems….

MySQL does not have a built-in command to execute shell commands like Microsoft SQL Server does. Arbitrary commands can be executed on underlying database servers when the back-end database system is MySQL, PostgreSQL, or Microsoft SQL Server and the session user has the necessary privileges to abuse certain database features and architecture weaknesses.

On some database servers, you can use the database server to access the operating system. A SQL injection vulnerability could allow an attacker to gain full access to all data on a database server. SQL injection vulnerabilities can affect any website or web application that uses a SQL database such as MySQL, Oracle, SQL Server or others.

SQL injection is a network security vulnerability that allows an attacker to interfere with the queries that an application makes against its database. SQL injection is a code injection technique used to attack data-driven applications where malicious SQL statements are entered into input fields to be executed (such as SQL databases.

SQL injection forces an insecure database to execute insecure commands by injecting malicious code into SQL (Structured Query Language) database, the most commonly used language for database management. SQL is a query language designed to manage data stored in relational databases. In cases where the results of a SQL query and a SQL query are returned in application responses, an attacker could use a SQL injection vulnerability to extract data from other tables in the database. Most instances of SQL injection can be prevented by using parameterized queries (also known as prepared statements) instead of concatenating rows in the query.

For example, SQL Server uses + to concatenate strings in statements, while Oracle uses ||. SQL Server allows you to execute a batch or multiple SQL commands in one batch statement, or multiple SQL commands as long as they are separated by a semicolon (;), whereas Oracle and MySQL prohibit this. An attacker can use the SQL commands in the input to modify the SQL statements executed by the database server.

To perform a SQL Injection attack, an attacker must first find vulnerable user data on a web page or web application. Attackers can use vulnerable user input fields as well as databases to inject malicious code, gain access, and compromise systems. For example, an attacker can interrupt operations, change security settings, steal data, or compromise systems in a way that leaves open loopholes for future exploitation. Attackers can bypass the authentication and authorization of a web page or web application and obtain the contents of the entire SQL database.

The malicious backdoor allows attackers to access all files in the hosting account. Attackers can also use SQL injection to add, modify, and delete records throughout the SQL database. The attacker then uses privileges to impersonate a real user, gain access to the target resource, and perform various undetected tasks. Hackers can also install backdoors that allow them to access servers indefinitely.

Database or file injection - injecting code into a database or system file to give hackers access. A successful SQL injection vulnerability can read sensitive data from the database, modify database data (insert/update/delete), perform database management operations (such as shutting down the DBMS), extract the contents of specific files present in the DBMS file system, and in some cases next, the command is sent to the operating system. Most people know that SQL injection allows attackers to extract database records, obtain past login screens, and modify the contents of the database, thereby creating new users with administrative privileges.

SQL injections can modify, insert, and delete elements from a database, or lay the foundation for a denial of service attack. SQL injection attacks allow attackers to falsify identities, tamper with existing data, cause failure issues such as transaction reversals or balance changes, ensure full disclosure of all data in a system, destroy data or otherwise make it inaccessible, and become database server administrators . First-order SQL injection occurs when an application receives user input from an HTTP request and, in the process of processing that request, injects the input into the SQL request in an insecure manner.

We will look at several ways to inject different types of backdoors into a server through a SQL injection vulnerability. In this section, we will explain what SQL injections are, describe some common examples, explain how to find and exploit different types of SQL injection vulnerabilities, and summarize how to prevent SQL injections. Some of the core features of the SQL language are implemented in the same way across popular database platforms, so many ways to detect and exploit SQL injection vulnerabilities work the same way across different types of databases.

You can get information about the make and version of a database by scanning network ports on the server, listening to network traffic, or examining SQL-related error messages. You can find out details about a database using inference methods. After reviewing the responses received, the hacker can begin to identify potential vulnerabilities in the database. Instead of filtering for a specific user, an SQL injection such as OR 1 = 1 into a search string, login portal, or other input field can cause SQL to query the database for all information about EACH user.

Database injection is a common threat where text scattered across multiple records can be reassembled with a simple request for malicious commands. It is very common for malware to infiltrate the database and get uploaded to your WordPress site through posts, pages, comments, and other site content. SQL sits right behind the elegant storefront, taking your queries and translating them into code for the database.

SQL injection is primarily known as an attack vector for websites, but it can be used to attack any type of SQL database. Another major way hackers can gain access to your website database is to perform SQL injection attacks.

A SQL Injection vulnerability could allow an attacker to gain full access to all data on a database server. In cases where the results of a SQL query and a SQL query are returned in application responses, an attacker could use a SQL injection vulnerability to extract data from other tables in the database. Most instances of SQL injection can be prevented by using parameterized queries (also known as prepared statements) instead of concatenating rows in the query.

For example, SQL Server uses + to concatenate strings in statements, while Oracle uses ||. SQL Server allows you to execute a batch or multiple SQL commands in one batch statement, or multiple SQL commands as long as they are separated by a semicolon (;), whereas Oracle and MySQL prohibit this. While most SQL server implementations allow multiple statements to be executed in a single call in this way, some SQL APIs (such as the PHP mysql_query() function) do not allow this for security reasons. For example, if you have multiple WordPress installations on the same web server, create separate databases with limited user access.

On some database servers, you can use the database server to access the operating system. Typically, the MySQL database runs on a separate machine, and your web server (containing your website files and WordPress PHP code) communicates with the MySQL database over a network connection. As you can see, your database credentials are very close to the Internet, and the only thing protecting them is a web server configured to prevent certain files from being accessed as text.

Your website files usually do not contain sensitive user data, but if an attacker has the ability to read or modify your website files or source code, he can collect user data very easily and can even get your MySQL database login information, which will allow them to directly access your user data. Attackers can bypass the authentication and authorization of a web page or web application and obtain the contents of the entire SQL database. Attackers can also use SQL injection to add, modify, and delete records in a database.

SQL injection is a web security vulnerability that allows an attacker to interfere with the queries an application makes against its database. SQL injection is a code injection technique used to attack data-driven applications in which malicious SQL statements are entered into an input field to be executed (for example, a SQL injection vulnerability can affect any website or web application that uses a SQL database , such as MySQL, Oracle, SQL Server or others.

We will look at several ways to inject different types of backdoors into a server through a SQL injection vulnerability. It is useful to know the different ways to install backdoors. Let's now see how the backdoor can be inserted into the database.

We're going to take an application I already have that is vulnerable to SQL injection and use an existing vulnerability to inject a backdoor into the system. Now we will use the existing vulnerability to launch a backdoor to the system. Now remember, we're going to paste our PHP code so we can execute shell commands.

To execute operating system commands, we will need a command shell (CMD) or we will need to execute code that allows us to execute operating system commands. Now we will try to write our code on the server that will help us execute arbitrary OS commands on the server. I will be using 2 MySQL database built-in commands: one that writes arbitrary files and another that can be used to read arbitrary files.

You can also find any number of SQL database dumps (joking around with a Google hack while preparing this article, I came across a dump for a top level CMS developer website). Considering that you can go to Google right now and type in a search string that will return thousands of website usernames and passwords, you realize that SQL injection is not a mystery at all. Using SQL commands on search forms can potentially perform some extremely powerful operations, such as getting usernames and passwords, looking up a set of database fields and field names, and changing them.

You can get information about the make and version of a database by scanning network ports on the server, listening to network traffic, or examining SQL-related error messages. If a hacker knows that, for example, SQL Server 2000 has certain exploits, and knows the unique string thrown from that version in the results, one can focus on vulnerable websites.

Most people know that SQL injection allows attackers to extract database records, get past login screens, and modify the contents of the database, creating new users with administrative privileges. Limiting the database permissions used by the web application to only what is needed can help reduce the effectiveness of any SQL injection attacks that exploit any bugs in the web application. Developers can use ORM frameworks such as Hibernate [19], to build database queries in a safe and developer-friendly way.

To perform a SQL injection attack, an attacker must first find vulnerable user data in a web page or web application. Blind SQL injection is used when a web application is vulnerable to SQL injection, but the results of the injection are not visible to the attacker. SQL injection is a code injection technique used to attack data-driven applications in which malicious SQL statements are injected into an input field to be executed (for example, command injection is a technique used by a hacker to execute system commands on a server, usually through an application) . or some kind of GUI.

In code injection, an attacker injects custom code, which is then executed by an application or program, and command injection takes advantage of the functionality of the application that executes system commands. This can happen when an application provides the user with some kind of functionality related to the use of system commands. Composite SQLI is based on the fact that SQL statements consist of both the data used by the SQL statement and the commands that control the execution of the SQL statement.

An attacker can use the SQL commands in the input to modify the SQL statements executed by the database server. Therefore, an attacker can execute arbitrary SQL commands and queries against the database server through the application processing layer [2]. By using a chroot environment, you can restrict write access to the database server process (and child processes), thereby increasing server security.

A successful SQL injection attack can read sensitive data from a database, modify data (insert/modify/update/delete), execute administrative processes and extract the contents of a specific file present on the database server, and even run system-level operations. commands [3]. SQL injection attacks allow attackers to falsify identities, tamper with existing data, cause failure issues such as transaction reversals or balance changes, ensure full disclosure of all data in a system, destroy data or otherwise make it inaccessible, and become database server administrators . Most people know that SQL injection allows attackers to extract database records, get past login screens, and modify the contents of the database, creating new users with administrative privileges.

For example, in a financial application, an attacker can use SQL Injection to change a balance, reverse transactions, or transfer money to their account. Attackers can bypass the authentication and authorization of a web page or web application and obtain the contents of the entire SQL database. Some approaches analyze the application and use heuristics or information flow analysis to detect code that may be vulnerable to an SQL injection attack.

As long as the data submitted by the user is not properly validated by the application, the attack itself will succeed if the data is inserted along with a legitimate SQL query. If the data submitted by the user is not properly validated, an attacker can use this request and bypass the login screen by simply sending specially crafted variables. The results of the malicious SQL query will be merged with the original query results.

A false positive occurs when the application server's security mechanism fails to stop a malicious web request and the SQL injection request is sent to the database server for execution. In some cases, the attacker will get lucky and execute the phpinfo() function. When the system is allowed to execute unintentional commands, an attacker can take over the server and get a shell, as we demonstrated with the popular Netcat tool.

If this is not possible, you need to be more careful, otherwise, by executing remote commands through the application server, an attacker can compromise the database even without permission. Restricting database permissions used by a web application to only those required can help reduce the effectiveness of any SQL injection attacks that exploit any bugs in the web application. I'll show you how SQL injection enables anyone to execute arbitrary commands using the standard functions provided by the MySQL database.

I will use Damn Vulnerable Web Application (DVWA) as part of Metasploitable 2 (Vulnerable Virtual Machine) to simulate command injection. The site runs on Linux, but the same approach can be applied to Windows servers using Windows commands. If this Webmin feature is enabled, an attacker can use it to control the Webmin installation by adding a shell command with `` | . " in the HTTP request sent to the Webmin server.

Once the computer running Webmin is compromised, attackers can use it to launch attacks against remote Unix-based systems. The backdoor mechanism was discovered in Webmin, a popular web application used by system administrators to manage Unix-based remote systems such as Linux, FreeBSD or OpenBSD servers, as well as Unix-based remote systems such as Linux, FreeBSD or OpenBSD Linux. server. The vulnerability could allow an unauthenticated attacker to execute code on a server running the Webmin application.

Malicious redirects use FTP, SFTP, wp-admin, and other protocols to create backdoors in WordPress installations and inject redirect code into websites. Attackers use input to unknowingly send malicious code, usually browser-side scripts, to end users.

Better Protection of Login and Password Information

For example, there are several ways to protect your login page from attacks and hide it from strangers. In addition, there are ways to force other users of your site to use strong passwords. You also need to make sure that everyone who has access to your site has equally strong passwords.

You need to protect yourself from intrusions that may occur due to the use of weak passwords. A weak password on your team can leave your website vulnerable to data loss, so be prepared for anyone with access.

You can make it harder to use by using a stronger password unique to your website. WordPress users generate more complex passwords to eliminate the possibility of online brute force attacks. Having a longer password makes it harder for hackers to use brute force attacks to get into your WordPress site. Brute force attacks can easily target WordPress sites with weak passwords, so it's important to use unique login details.

Therefore, hackers cannot even access the WordPress login page without another password. Try password protecting your wp-login.php so that only site administrators and site owners can access it. You can also use the code snippet below to restrict access to wp-admin instead of password protection.

Another way to combat this type of security threat is to protect the entire wp-admin directory with a different password. Protect brings up the login page, in addition to displaying your username and password, it also asks for a second password to grant access.

The Users section of your WordPress dashboard allows you to create strong and random passwords, so there is no excuse for using a weak password. It's tempting to use a password that you know will always be easy to remember. Many people end up using the same password in all places in order to remember their login information. With so many websites, databases, and programs requiring passwords, it's hard to keep track of them.

We know it's hard to find a new password for every site and app you visit often, not to mention how frustrating it is to remember what they all are, but having a strong password can be critical to protecting your account. records. .

Using a different password for your hosting account and for each FTP user in the account adds several layers of security to your hosting environment.

None of the passwords allow the user to access your contact and billing information in the account profile, so your personal information remains secure. Also refrain from using any personal information in your password. Don't use your birthday or pet's name; make it completely illegible. Do not share your password with anyone, for any reason. Passwords should not be shared with anyone, including students, faculty, or employees.

Even if you don't deal with credit card numbers on your website, that doesn't mean you shouldn't protect your users' privacy. Blocking the admin area and access to WordPress is a good way to increase your security. If you want to further strengthen your login process, you should consider implementing two-factor authentication to secure your WordPress website. We've implemented sophisticated internal security measures for the login process to prevent targeted attacks, and added options such as restricted user password and two-factor authentication to ensure easy login without sacrificing security.

Two-factor authentication means that in addition to entering a password, users need to enter a code generated by a mobile app or other device to access your website. With two-factor authentication enabled, stealing your password will no longer be enough to give criminals access to your account, as they'll also need to enter a security token, also known as a captcha, that you will delete from the app. Smartphone or email account, depending on how you set it up.

In order to access your website, a person must have your username and password to log in, they must have access to your phone, and they must know how to log into your phone. For example, hackers can steal user login details and passwords. So they can target a wider range of websites and gain access with the same type of malware or virus. This means that hackers can test many of these passwords at the same time, making it easier to access your website, rather than cautiously trying password after password.

This may seem obvious, but you will be surprised at how often site administrators use a short and very simple password to enter their personal account. If the password you use to log into WordPress is the same as the password you use for social media, streaming and shopping services, or banking institutions, you should change it immediately.

After installing and configuring one of the above plugins, you will usually have an extra field on the WordPress login page for you to enter a security code. This is one of the reasons why at Kinsta, on new WordPress installations, we enforce a strong wp-admin login password (as shown in the one-click installation process below). Change your password after three months or earlier and try again.

There is a wealth of information out there for consumers, families, and individuals about password protection, proper protection of desktops, laptops, and mobile devices from hackers, malware, and other threats, and best practices for using the Internet safely. We've put together 101 data protection tips to help you protect your passwords, financial information, and personal information online. No one can prevent any kind of identity theft, but by using these tips, you can help make your personal information a little more "personal" online—and in this age of digital connectivity, that's what you should be striving for. Using strong passwords and advanced authentication methods can help protect your personal information.

If you have too many passwords to remember, consider using password management software that can help you create strong personal passwords and keep them safe. It's better to create a unique password than to use the same password on multiple sites - a password manager tool can help you keep track of it. That's why you use unique passwords for each online account.

By choosing a unique password for each account, hackers who break into one account cannot use it to access all the others. Too often, if one account has been hacked, your data is no longer secure in other accounts that use the same login information, especially if you use the same password for multiple services. Avoid using the same password for multiple accounts. Using the same password for multiple accounts makes passwords easier to remember, but can also have a ripple effect that allows an attacker to gain unauthorized access to multiple systems.

Strong passwords are the key to your online security, but the trick is to create different passwords that you can actually remember otherwise you might get into the bad habit of using the same login credentials for multiple accounts. The single best way to prevent the domino effect of a data breach is to use a strong unique password for each of your online accounts. Creating a unique and secure password for every account is not a job for a human.

Your Microsoft account password, you need a specially configured physical security key to log in to your computer, so even if someone guesses or cracks your password, they won't be able to log in. We're talking about real old-fashioned paper, not electronic documents like Word files or Google spreadsheets, because if someone logs into your computer or online account, they can also access this electronic password file.

If a thief steals your password, you can still prevent them from accessing your account using two-factor authentication (also known as two-step verification or 2FA), a security measure that requires you to enter a second piece of information that only you have (usually one-time code) before the application or service comes in. Some accounts require two or more credentials to log into your account, providing additional security. Hackers might try to use the same username and password combination to log into a banking website or a large online store.

Password managers are not for everyone, and some leading security experts, such as the Electronic Frontier Foundation, suggest that storing your login information on a physical piece of paper or notepad is a viable way to keep track of your credentials. Keeping your passwords, financial information, and other personal information secure and protected from outside attackers has long been a business priority, but it's becoming increasingly important that consumers and individuals follow data protection guidelines and usage practices. . Practical advice from the federal government and the high-tech industry to help you guard against Internet scams, protect your computer, and protect your personal information.

Once your computers, tablets, and mobile phones are secure, take steps to protect your accounts, especially those that contain personal information, such as your banking, email, and social media accounts. If you store secure data on a flash drive or external hard drive, make sure it is encrypted and locked.

You can encrypt your Windows or macOS hard drive with BitLocker (Windows) or FileVault (macOS), encrypt any USB drive containing sensitive information, and use a VPN to encrypt web traffic. The best way to protect sensitive information from malware is to encrypt it. .

After visiting a website where you have entered sensitive information (such as credit card or bank or brokerage account numbers and passwords), consider clearing your web browser's cache file, as sensitive information is often also stored in the browser. My advice is to only keep files that you need to access frequently and avoid entering files that contain passwords or personal information (PII) for various online accounts, such as credit card numbers, ID numbers, home addresses, etc.

If you reuse passwords for more than one secure computer, account, website, or other system, please note that more than one computer, those secure computers, accounts, websites, and systems will only be as secure as the least secure the system on which you used this password. Reusing passwords or using the same password everywhere is like carrying a key that unlocks your home, car, office, briefcase, and safe. Passwords are used to protect user accounts, but the wrong password, if hacked, can put the entire network at risk.

In cases where a password needs to be written down, it should be kept in a safe place and properly destroyed when it is no longer needed (see Data Protection Guidelines). Extended passwords are usually the easiest way to increase password strength.

LastPass and 1Password can generate passwords, monitor accounts for security breaches, recommend weak password changes, and sync passwords between computers and phones. When you store information in the cloud, you are trusting others to keep that information safe.

How to Prevent Cross Site Scripting

Cross-site scripting attacks work by injecting code (usually client-side scripting such as JavaScript) into the output of a web application. Malicious activity on trusted websites. A cross-site scripting (XSS) attack is a type of injection in which malicious scripts are injected into a secure and trustworthy website. Cross-site scripting or "XSS" is a form of attack performed by injecting untrusted data, such as malicious JavaScript code, into a victim's web browser.

Cross-site scripting (XSS) is a security vulnerability that allows a user to modify code provided by an application to a user that is running in the user's web browser. If an attacker can use an XSS vulnerability in a web page to run arbitrary JavaScript in a user's browser, the security of the affected website or web application and its users will be compromised. The attacker seeks to execute malicious scripts in the victim's web browser by injecting malicious code into a legitimate web page or web application. The attacker can then enter a malicious string that will be used on the web page and treated as source code by the victim's browser.

Attackers can use embedded scripts to change the content of a website or even redirect the browser to a different web page, such as one that contains malicious code. An attacker injects a payload into a website's database by submitting a vulnerable form with malicious JavaScript content. In this type of attack, an attacker injects malicious JavaScript into a website, causing the browser to execute the script and perform the actions specified by the attacker in the script. In this particular case, the attacker injects code into the website where it is stored and inadvertently distributes it to any user.

In a Stored XSS attack, the user receives malicious code as part of the vulnerable website's response to a legitimate request. This is an example of a reflex XSS attack, as the malicious script is immediately "reflected" to the user making the request. The injected script is reflected by the web server - in an error message or search results - and navigates to the vulnerable website, repelling the attack on the victim's browser. In some cases, browser-side scripting can also lead to this vulnerability, allowing an attacker to exploit it without the target user making a request to the web application.

An XSS attack occurs when an attacker uses a web application to send malicious code, usually in the form of a browser-side script, to another end user. Attacks that exploit XSS vulnerabilities can steal data, control user sessions, execute malicious code, or be used as part of phishing scams. Attackers use XSS to create malicious code that can be redirected to another user and then run by an unsuspecting browser. XSS vulnerabilities provide an ideal breeding ground for expanding attacks to more serious ones.

The variety of XSS-based attacks is almost limitless, but they typically involve passing personal data such as cookies or other session information to the attacker, redirecting the victim to web content controlled by the attacker, or performing other operations on users' computers under the guise of a vulnerability. . A typical attack involves distributing malicious content to users in order to steal data or credentials. A successful attack results in information theft, session hijacking, malware, loss of sensitive information, and display of malicious ads. Other attacks require the attacker to convince or trick the user into downloading a malicious link first, perhaps through an email, instant messaging, message, or forum comment.

When a user is tricked into clicking a malicious link, submitting a specially crafted form, or even simply browsing a malicious website, the injected code spreads to the vulnerable website, mirroring the user's browser attack in the user's browser. By injecting malicious script into unprotected or unvalidated input provided by the browser, the attacker causes the script to be returned by the application and executed in the browser. Attackers can insert malicious scripts into configuration file fields, and when other users access the configuration file, their browsers automatically execute code. Cross-site scripting attacks can occur anywhere a potentially malicious user is allowed to post unregulated material on a trusted website for use by other legitimate users.

XSS attacks work even when the site is viewed over an SSL connection, because the script is executed in the context of a "secure" site, and browsers cannot distinguish between legitimate and malicious content served by a web application. Site scripting is a web application vulnerability that allows an attacker to inject and execute malicious client-side code in a victim's browser in a legitimate web application. Cross-site scripting, a type of security vulnerability in which attackers insert malicious client-side code into web pages, has existed since the 1990s, and most major websites such as Google,

Yahoo, and Facebook have suffered from cross-site scripting attacks. shortcomings in some aspects. In a DOM-based XSS attack, the vulnerability resides in browser-side scripting code and can be exploited without any interaction with the server by altering the browser environment of an unsuspecting victim.

Typically, XSS attacks target the server side, but with DOM-based attacks, scripts run entirely on the client side and manipulate the Document Object Model (DOM) rather than HTML code. DOM-based XSS (also called "XSS Type 0" in some texts) is an XSS attack in which the payload is executed by changing the DOM "environment" in the victim's browser. Used by the original client-side script, so the client-side code runs "unexpectedly". For example, in a contact form, an attacker can use the form to submit a malicious payload, and once the server user/application administrator opens the attacker-submitted form through the server application, the attacker's payload is executed.

Cross-Site Scripting (XSS) Overview of the three main types of Cross-Site Scripting (XSS) attacks: reflection, archive, and DOM-based. The three main types of cross-site scripting (XSS) attacks are reflection, archive, and DOM-based. Use trusted types to prevent DOM-based cross-site scripting vulnerabilities. Your application may be vulnerable to reflected/stored XSS and XSS DOM.

In order to detect the possibility of XSS DOM, a client-side attack must be simulated in the user's browser using a web application scanner such as Acunetix (which has a DOM-based XSS scanner capability). In a DOM-based XSS attack, the site/application Programs have vulnerable client-side scripts that send malicious scripts to the target browser. When an attacker uses a web application to send malicious code (usually in the form of a browser-side script) to another end user, it XSS attacks can occur.

Stored XSS occurs when malicious input is permanently stored on the server and returned to the user in a vulnerable web application. Once an attacker manages to send malicious content to the server and that content appears on a web page unfiltered, all users become potential victims. A common defense against archival XSS attacks is to sanitize input to the front-end and back-end of an application. Attackers typically exploit stored XSS payloads by injecting XSS payloads into popular pages of a site, or by passing links to victims to trick them into viewing pages that contain stored XSS payloads, stored XSS payloads.

Attackers use XSS to create malicious code that can be redirected to another user and then run by an unsuspecting browser. A DOM-based XSS attack can be successfully executed even if the server does not embed malicious code in a web page by exploiting a vulnerability in JavaScript running in a web browser. In a DOM-based XSS attack, the vulnerability resides in the browser. is a third-party script code and can be used without any interaction with the server, by changing the browser environment of unsuspecting victims. In some cases, browser-side scripting can also lead to this vulnerability, allowing an attacker to exploit it without being prompted by the targeted user of the web application.

Unlike reflection attacks that send malicious scripts from the target, users of a vulnerable website or web application may be vulnerable during normal interactions with the vulnerable site/application. As you can see, the main difference between a reflective XSS attack and a persistent XSS attack is that a persistent XSS attack treats all users of a vulnerable site/application as the target of the attack.

Because the XSS runs inside the victim's web browser, the attacker's code is executed at the user's privilege level. An attacker can insert malicious scripts into profile fields, and when other users visit the profile, their browser automatically executes the code. An attacker can run JavaScript of their choice on the victim's machine, so XSS can be used to execute various security threats and/or used in conjunction with other web vulnerabilities to exploit a serious security vulnerability. Cross-site scripting, or "XSS", is a form of attack carried out by injecting untrusted data, such as malicious JavaScript code, into the victim's web browser.

Attackers have been exploiting cross-site scripting vulnerabilities since the early 2000s, and XSS has been listed as one of the top ten critical security threats for OWASP web applications since 2004. XSS attacks are still a problem. Cross Site Scripting is a web application vulnerability that allows an attacker to inject and execute malicious client-side code in the victim's browser of a legitimate web application. DOM-based XSS (also called "XSS Type 0" in some texts) is an XSS attack in which the payload is executed by changing the

DOM "environment" in the victim's browser. Used by the original client-side script, so the client-side code behaves in an "unexpected" way.

Typically, XSS attacks target the server side, but with DOM-based attacks, scripts run entirely on the client side and manipulate the Document Object Model (DOM) rather than HTML code. DOM-based XSS vulnerabilities arise when the DOM is used to create dynamic content that contains user input that can be processed without validation. For example, if client-site JavaScript modifies the DOM tree of a web page based on input fields or GET parameters, without validating the input, malicious code may be executed.

In the stored XSS example, a malicious script may have been sent through an input field to a web server that did not perform adequate validation and permanently stored the script in a database. This is an example of a reflected XSS attack, as the malicious script is immediately "reflected" to the requesting user. The diagram below assumes that the attacker has discovered an archived cross-site scripting vulnerability in the target web application and can trick or guarantee that the victim will visit a page containing the archived payload.

The definition of an XSS client, any vulnerability or attack that does not use a web server to deliver a payload to a victim is an XSS client. The flaws that allow XSS attacks to succeed are fairly common and can occur anywhere a web application uses user input in the output it generates without validation or encoding.

DOM-based XSS vulnerabilities typically occur when JavaScript fetches data from an attacker-controlled source (such as a URL) and passes it to a dynamic executable sink (such as eval() or innerHTML). The key term DOM-based cross-site scripting occurs when data from a user-controlled source (such as a username or a redirect URL extracted from a URL fragment) arrives at a sink (such as a function such as eval() or a property setter), e.g. . innerHTML that can execute arbitrary JavaScript code. If usage is completely unavoidable, the best way to prevent DOM-based XSS is to use a safe output method (sink) to prevent any malicious inline code from running. As with archiving XSS, to prevent DOM attacks and reflection attacks, developers should implement data validation and avoid viewing raw user input, whether they are connected to the server or not.

Another way to prevent XSS attacks is to use the Crashtest Security Suite XSS tool, a web-based vulnerability scanner with a 14-day free trial, where you will find any vulnerabilities you may be exposed to.

Encryption Basics

EFS In Windows Explorer, right-click a file or folder. Usually, however, after installation you will be able to find the files and folders you want to protect in the Windows file manager and right-click on those files to choose to use. If you use 7-zip or Microsoft Office to encrypt your files , Windows 10 is likely still hiding one or more temporary copies of unencrypted files on the drive. If you encrypt a single file with EFS, your computer will store an unencrypted version of the file in temporary storage so that hackers can still access it.

If the laptop is lost or stolen and the files or drive are not encrypted, it's easy for a thief to steal your information, so it's a good idea to encrypt sensitive data, if not the entire hard drive. USB drives must also be encrypted because when you copy files from an encrypted drive to a USB drive, the files may be decrypted automatically.

This means it's time for encryption, where a drive, file or folder is scrambled (encrypted) so that the drive becomes unreadable and only someone with the correct key can decrypt it. Now that your file or folder is encrypted, you don't need a password to access it, except the one you use to access your Windows profile when you turn on your computer. Other user accounts on your computer will not be able to access the files contained in the encrypted folder.

You can choose to encrypt just this folder, or you can encrypt all subfolders and folder files. A window will appear asking if you want to encrypt the selected folder or folder, subfolders and files. Select Apply Changes to Encryption-Only Folder or Apply Changes to This Folder, Subfolders, and Files, then click OK. Click the pop-up message "Backing up the file encryption key." Select your preferences and click OK. You can also backup the file's encryption key.

To decrypt your files, right-click on the file, select Properties > Advanced in the Advanced attribute, uncheck Encrypt content to protect data, click OK, then click Apply, click OK, and all. If you created an archive to protect files or folders on your system, you should go to the section called "Delete all possible unencrypted copies of a file" once you've finished encrypting the files and follow the instructions there to make sure there are no unencrypted copies of things , lying around where some curious person might find them. When creating a file archive, the contents can be encrypted by specifying a password.

This is another free and open source program that allows you to use password protection, as well as encrypt files and folders in compressed archives. Third party software allows you to save all your personal files in a password protected container.

In the Microsoft Office suite, you can password-protect Office files such as Word documents or PowerPoint presentations with built-in encryption. In most versions of Windows, files and folders cannot be password protected, so they must be encrypted, or a third-party password protector must be used to protect folders from cybercrime in Windows 7, 8, and 10 . You can also encrypt individual Microsoft Office files from within its application, although this is better for occasional human use than protection from serious intruders.

If you're a Windows 10 Home user, you'll need to encrypt your files with a third-party encryption app. The easiest and quickest way to securely encrypt files on your hard drive is to use Windows' own encryption tools.

If you want to encrypt the drive to prevent unauthorized access, it's built into the Pro version of Windows, so it's worth using something that can be "smashed and grabbed" by a car, like a laptop. You can use it to encrypt drives, as well as shred and permanently delete files.

Entire Disk or Entire Disk EncryptionA is transparent to users and does not require them to store files in a special location on the disk because all files, folders and volumes are encrypted. Encrypting individual files and foldersA is acceptable if you have a relatively small number of business documents stored on your computer, and this is better than no encryption at all. It is available for Windows, Linux and Mac OS X. Veracrypt will allow you to encrypt individual files in an encrypted container protected by a passphrase.

The WINZIP tool is used to encrypt data on computers such as PCs, laptops and servers in a compressed .zip folder file with password protection to ensure a high level of data security for sensitive data files. The built-in Bit Locker supports on-the-fly encryption methodology, which means data encryption, including data files, folders, free space, metadata, image and media files, email backup, etc. AxCrypt is a great free encryption utility that allows you to users to encrypt all files in a folder and does not allow viewing of these files unless the passphrase (password) is known.

How to encrypt files and folders in Windows 10 There are two easy ways to encrypt files and folders in Windows 10: using Microsoft Encrypting File

System (EFS) or BitLocker. The file encryption process in Windows can make files inaccessible to other standard user accounts or to unauthenticated logon processes on the computer. If you only have one partition on the entire drive (as we did on this computer), a very affordable alternative will allow you to choose only the encrypt system partition option.

Here's how to encrypt files on your Android device, whether you want to encrypt everything on your Android device or just certain files. If your Android phone or device does not support full encryption, you can always download an app that encrypts individual files or folders. Not all Android phones, tablets or devices will have full disk encryption as an option. Without the key provided by your password and the Android device that encrypted the data on your device, all anyone can get is a jumble of numbers and letters.

Fortunately, the Android operating system comes with a handy security feature that encrypts your device from head to toe, locking down personal information so recovery is nearly impossible. Encryption doesn't just stop someone from accessing the information on your mobile device. Most modern Android phones don't have built-in hardware-based data encryption, which means you have to rely on third-party apps to protect your text messages, emails, and other important information. While Android 5.0 and higher does not require the user to activate the lock screen to enable device encryption, it is recommended because encrypted phones without some form of authentication are simply not secure.

How to Enable Encryption on Android Enabling device encryption on your Android device is a very simple process, and many phones even enable it right away. Unlike iPhones, Android devices don't automatically encrypt data stored on them when you set a passcode, but this is easy to enable if you're using Android Gingerbread 2.3.4 or higher. The downside of encrypting your mobile data is that, at least on Android devices, it takes longer to access your device because every time you do this, the data is decrypted. After encryption is complete, your Android device will reboot and Android will ask you for a password to decrypt the vault.

Once encryption is complete, you can enter your PIN or password and start using your phone. Before starting the encryption process, you will be prompted to connect your phone to charge it, eliminating the possibility of disconnecting the device during the process. If your device is not encrypted, you can start the process by clicking Encrypt Phone.

If you haven't already, you'll be prompted to set a lock screen PIN or password, which you'll need to enter when you turn on your phone or unlock it to access new encrypted files. When the phone is locked, encryption is enabled, so even if attackers bypass the screen, all they find is encrypted data where encrypted files appear. Everything on iPhone is locked as soon as you set up a PIN, Touch ID fingerprint, or Face ID — The PIN, fingerprint, or face acts as a key to unlock the encryption, so you can read your messages and view your files as soon as your the phone will be unlocked.

You probably don't think about encryption every day. It means that if someone steals your phone, they won't get anything without the PIN. Without the encryption key, attackers will not be able to access the data, although there are more advanced hacking methods to do this.

If you reboot the device before choosing to decrypt, the key will be lost and you will lose access to protected files on the microSD card. This also means that resetting the device to factory settings will destroy the encryption key used to decrypt the microSD card, making the data irrecoverable. Without completely removing the encryption, you will no longer be able to use the microSD card with other devices because the other phone or computer will not know the key.

Some devices also allow you to encrypt the contents of the SD card, but by default, Android only encrypts the internal memory. On the security settings screen of many phones, you can also choose to encrypt the SD card.

Like some Android phones, Windows 10 phones running the latest version of Windows 10 offer the option to encrypt the SD card. If you have a Windows Phone running Windows 10 Mobile, you can choose to encrypt your device or SD card. Some Android phones allow users to encrypt their SD card through their device.

Shared files cannot be encrypted with Android's default method because they are first decrypted on the device, and the keys cannot be replayed for use on other devices. To encrypt files on your Android device, you will use the Andrognito app, which uses a 256-bit encryption algorithm to keep your files secure.

Aside from logging in, you can usually work fine on Android as long as the encryption process doesn't slow down your device too much. If your device is rooted, which means you've been granted full administrator (or root access) access to the Android subsystem, you can't encrypt it right away.

First, encryption can slow down your phone's performance and cause your device to take much longer to boot than usual. Even on high-end devices, booting an encrypted phone can take about 5 minutes.

In order to access or read data from an encrypted file, you need to have a secret key or, more simply, a password that will help you in decrypting the files. The data in encrypted files is stored in the form of complex code that is difficult to crack in a reasonable amount of time. While most data can be easily stored, sensitive data must be encrypted in the database. In any case, all database servers and other server connections and settings must be encrypted.

If you need to protect documents from _local_ users on the server's host system, you will need to start the server as something other than ``none" and set permissions on both confidential documents and server scripts so that they are not public. . . . If you don't check your server environment, for example if your website is hosted on GitHub Pages or similar platforms, you won't be able to use full or complete (strict) implementation, which means that even if your users see HTTPS in the address bar, traffic will not completely go to the encrypted source server. Once you have enabled HSTS on your domain, you can be sure that once someone loads your site over HTTPS, they will only be able to access it over HTTPS from now on. If you're in control of your server, you can quickly deploy HTTPS on your site with Let us Encrypt.

We recommend that you use HTTPS to protect users' connections to your website, regardless of its content. If you are not connected to a secure HTTPS website, traffic between the VPN company's servers and the website is not encrypted. You can use a virtual private network or VPN to encrypt your internet traffic. Since business activities have a fundamental need for secure transmission over the Internet, there is great interest in developing schemes for encrypting data in transit between browsers and servers.

Learning how to encrypt a website by enabling HTTPS is a must, especially for companies that want to provide users with a safe and secure online experience. As part of enabling HTTPS for your website, you must obtain a security certificate. No matter what server infrastructure you have, CloudFlare can help you secure your SSL certificates for free. Automated software running on a web server can interact with Let us Encrypt to easily obtain certificates, configure security for use, and handle updates automatically.

Secure Let us Encrypt will serve as a platform to promote TLS security best practices both on the CA side and by helping website operators to ensure their servers are properly secured. After setting up the server and running our website on HTTPS, I highly recommend checking its security configuration with Qualys SSL Server Test. The SSL protocol includes means for server authentication (server authentication on the client), encryption of transmitted data, and optional client authentication (client identity verification on the server). HTTP Secure (HTTPS) only truly protects information security in one direction: from the client to the server, because information encrypted with the public key can only be decrypted with the private key; therefore, only the server can decrypt it.

Only someone with the correct encryption key (such as a password) can decrypt your data. This security method, better known as encryption, masks digital information so that only those with the correct encryption key can decrypt it. Encryption alone cannot provide integrity, but by protecting imperative data, it can protect data from a hacker that can be used by companies to make business decisions. Hackers can access and use your personal data from your device and use it in an unauthorized way where data encryption can be demonstrated to protect the privacy of your data.

Some common data that needs to be encrypted include user IDs, email addresses, passwords, social security numbers, birth details, credit card details, password prompt responses, personal medical records, chat and private messages, financial and banking information data. If you need to encrypt credentials in code, make sure they are encrypted and the private/public key is stored somewhere securely. You can collaborate with your team members and allow them to open files encrypted with a specific password.

You can also encrypt your files before uploading them to cloud storages; just to be extremely careful, no one can access it. After copying a file to secure storage or creating an encrypted version of it, be sure to delete the unencrypted original. Your files cannot be decrypted on Encrypto's servers, especially since it uses AES-256 keys.

You can go the extra mile and inform your users of the remaining holes, or you can opt out, encrypt the server and just use SSL to transfer data (and possibly suggest to users that they encrypt their data locally first, for every opportunity). This will depend on the sensitivity of the data or message, the size of the data files, how the data is sent (e-mail, FTP), and the recipient's preferred encryption standards. There are several encryption methods, algorithms or codes used in data encoding that designers and developers can use.

Incorporating encryption into the design and development process can help you end up with a product that is free of fines and sanctions. If your server's security is compromised, it can lead to anything from injecting spam ads into a corporate website to intercepting and stealing user data when submitting forms. The files in the secure folder are automatically encrypted when you log out, and it's one of the few folders that supports public key encryption.

- End -

Don't miss out!

Visit the website below and you can sign up to receive emails whenever Warren H. Lau publishes a new book. There's no charge and no obligation.

https://books2read.com/r/B-A-OZQW-NGEHC

BOOKS 2 READ

Connecting independent readers to independent writers.

About the Author

Warren H. Lau is currently C.E.O. of a tech firm, and has many years of experience in overseeing web-based development projects.

The main duty of his job is to design and oversee the development of usable websites, mobile sites and mobile apps that are user friendly and immune to cyberattacks; at the same time, lead the marketing team to achieve business success.

Before Warren H. Lau begins his career in the technology industry, he spent more than ten years in the investment career, and succeeded through a combined application of fundamental, technical and news analysis. He summarized all his knowledge and experience and published his investment book series: "Winning Strategies of Professional Investment".

About the Publisher

INPress International is a global publication organization that focuses on knowledges and topics where the traditional schooling system do not provide. Our Mission is to build a more humanistic, fair and peaceful future through our publication works.